Build Better Chatbots

A Complete Guide to Getting Started with Chatbots

Rashid Khan

Anik Das

Apress®

Build Better Chatbots

Rashid Khan
Bangalore, Karnataka, India

Anik Das
Bangalore, Karnataka, India

ISBN-13 (pbk): 978-1-4842-3110-4
https://doi.org/10.1007/978-1-4842-3111-1

ISBN-13 (electronic): 978-1-4842-3111-1

Library of Congress Control Number: 2017963347

Cover image by Freepik (`www.freepik.com`)

Managing Director: Welmoed Spahr
Editorial Director: Todd Green
Acquisitions Editor: Celestin Suresh John
Development Editor: Matthew Moodie
Technical Reviewer: Puneet Jindal
Coordinating Editor: Sanchita Mandal
Copy Editor: Kim Wimpsett
Compositor: SPi Global
Indexer: SPi Global
Artist: SPi Global

Distributed to the book trade worldwide by Springer Science+Business Media New York, 233 Spring Street, 6th Floor, New York, NY 10013. Phone 1-800-SPRINGER, fax (201) 348-4505, e-mail `orders-ny@springer-sbm.com`, or visit `www.springeronline.com`. Apress Media, LLC is a California LLC and the sole member (owner) is Springer Science + Business Media Finance Inc (SSBM Finance Inc). SSBM Finance Inc is a **Delaware** corporation.

For information on translations, please e-mail `rights@apress.com`, or visit `www.apress.com/rights-permissions`.

Apress titles may be purchased in bulk for academic, corporate, or promotional use. eBook versions and licenses are also available for most titles. For more information, reference our Print and eBook Bulk Sales web page at `www.apress.com/bulk-sales`.

Any source code or other supplementary material referenced by the author in this book is available to readers on GitHub via the book's product page, located at `www.apress.com/978-1-4842-3110-4`. For more detailed information, please visit `www.apress.com/source-code`.

Printed on acid-free paper

Contents

About the Authors

Rashid Khan is an author and entrepreneur. He cofounded Yellow Messenger with Anik Das, Raghu Ravinutala, and Jaya Kishore. Previously he worked at EdegeVerve Systems Ltd., where he built back ends to support IoT devices. In addition, he is the author of the book *Learning IoT with Particle Photon and Electron* (Packt Publishing, 2016).

Anik Das is an open source enthusiast and an entrepreneur at heart. He cofounded Yellow Messenger with Rashid Rhan, Raghu Ravinutala, and Jaya Kishore. He is a frequent contributor to a lot of Python and JavaScript projects on GitHub. He is also a contributor to Django-LibSpark, a Python library designed to enable Django to access Apache Spark in a UI.

CHAPTER 1

■ ■ ■

Introduction to Chatbots

Welcome to the *Build Better Chatbots* book. Do you remember the last time you had to call a toll-free number for support or customer service? Do you remember the long wait time on the phone before you could even talk about your issue and then realizing somehow you chose the wrong button option leading you to the wrong department? We have had this experience, and that's why we created a chatbot for enterprises to use to help resolve customer questions more easily and in an interface that many people, especially millennials, are getting more accustomed to using: chat. In this book, we will take you through the history of chatbots, including when they were invented and how they became popular. We will also show how to build a chatbot for your next project. After completing this book, you will know how to deploy applications with a chat interface on platforms such as Facebook Messenger, Skype, and so on, which automatically respond to user queries without any human intervention.

The book is divided into five chapters, with topics ranging from the technical to the business perspective. If you are a rock-star developer who can't wait to build a Hello World example, then Chapters 2 to 4 are designed for you. Chapter 5 is business and monetization oriented, so if you already have a chatbot or have heard about chatbots and want to explore further, then Chapter 5 is the place to be. For the best reading experience, follow the chronological order of Chapters 1 to 5.

In this chapter, we will start by covering the chatbot ecosystem, the journey of chatbots through multiple decades, and the various open platforms today where you can deploy your chatbot.

■ **Fact**   The term *chatterbot* was first used in 1994 and was originally coined by Michael Mauldin, the creator of Verbot (Verbal Robot) Julia.

What Are Chatbots?

The classic definition of a *chatbot* is a computer program that processes natural-language input from a user and generates smart and relative responses that are then sent back to the user. Currently, chatbots are powered by rules-driven engines or artificial intelligent (AI) engines that interact with users via a text-based interface primarily. These are

© Rashid Khan and Anik Das 2018   1
R. Khan and A. Das, *Build Better Chatbots*, https://doi.org/10.1007/978-1-4842-3111-1_1

independent computer programs that can be plugged into any of the multiple messaging platforms that have opened to developers via APIs such as Facebook Messenger, Slack, Skype, Microsoft Teams, and so on.

With the advancement of voice technology in recent years, companies such as Google, Apple, and Amazon have debuted artificial intelligent agents for voice. Apple launched Siri, which comes on the iPhone, iPad, and macOS. Google launched Google Home, and Amazon launched Alexa, which are both physically devices for your home or office that can help you with tasks such as ordering a hired car, switching on/off your lights, playing your favorite tunes from Spotify, managing your calendars, and so on.

The technology behind chatbots is based on similar technology to voice-based assistants. All voice-based systems have the added complexity of converting the speech to text for any computer application to work with. The processing of the text from a chatbot or a voice-based system is done in the same way, and you will look at the underlying workflow and implement your own system in this book.

Journey of Chatbots

Let's start your journey of chatbots by looking at the history of chatbots. Chat as a medium has existed from the time computers have been in existence and has become one of the prominent mediums of communication in the last couple of decades. In this section of the chapter, we will cover the origin of chatbots and how the early computer scientists have always been excited about making a computer talk to a human in a natural way. We will also go into current developments in the industry that are facilitating the availability of chatbots on a large scale today. For a better understanding of the timeline of chatbots, see Figure 1-1.

Brief History of Chatbots

Even though *chatbot* seems to be a recent buzzword, they've been in existence since people developed a way to interact with computers. The first-ever chatbot was introduced even before the first personal computer was developed. It was named Eliza and was developed at the MIT Artificial Intelligence Laboratory by Joseph Weizenbaum in 1966. Eliza impersonated a psychotherapist. Eliza examined the keywords in the user input and triggered the rules of transformation of the output. This particular methodology of generating responses is still widely being used when building chatbots. After Eliza, Parry was written by psychiatrist Kenneth Colby, then at Stanford University, in an attempt to simulate a person with paranoid schizophrenia.

A.L.I.C.E., or simply Alicebot, was originally developed by Richard Wallace in 1995 and was inspired by Eliza. Although it failed to pass the Turing test, A.L.I.C.E. remained one of the strongest of its kind and was awarded the Loebner Prize, an annual competition of AI, three times.

■ **Note**   A *Turing test* is a test for intelligence in a computer wherein a human (sender) should not be able to distinguish between a machine (receiver) or another human (receiver) when replies from both are presented to the sender. The Turing test was designed by Alan Turing in 1950 in his paper "Computing Machinery and Intelligence" while working at the University of Manchester.

In the first decade of 21st century, SmarterChild was built by ActiveBuddy. It was the first attempt to create a chatbot that was able not only to provide entertainment but also to provide the user with more useful information such as stock information, sports scores, movie quotes, and much more. It lived inside AOL and Windows Live Messenger, with more than 30 million people using it. It was later acquired by Microsoft in 2007 for $46 million. SmarterChild is the precursor of Siri by Apple and S Voice by Samsung.

Siri is an intelligent personal assistant that was developed as a side project by SRI International and later adopted by Apple into its iOS 5 for iPhone. It's been an integral part of the iOS ecosystem. Siri allows users to engage in random conversations while providing useful information regarding the weather, stocks, and movie tickets. Tech giants like Samsung and Google have also followed in the footsteps of Apple by developing their own AI assistants, S Voice and Google Allo, respectively.

There are also voice-powered home assistants like Amazon Alexa and Google Home, which are another representation of chatbots.

Recent Developments of Chatbots

When looking at history, companies have always built their own individual AI-powered chatbots to serve the purpose of their end users. In recent years, this trend has changed, with Telegram opening its bot platform in June 2015, allowing developers to make chatbots serving users with numerous services such as polls, news, games, integration, and entertainment. In addition, Slack, a cross-platform team collaboration software application, announced *bot users* in December 2015. Slack launching its bot users platform was a catalyst in pushing other companies to start investing in this new channel of user engagement.

As one of the biggest players in this market, Facebook released its Messenger platform in April 2016 during the F8 developer conference. Although Facebook was a bit late to the party, it had the most impact on the buzz of chatbots. The opportunity to reach 1 billion active users via Messenger played a major role in this.

To name a few more, Skype, Kik, and WeChat are the other major players in messaging that have released their platforms for developers to publish chatbots.

To summarize, if you picture the journey of chatbots from the 1960s to now, you can see that what was once a fantasy of being able to communicate with a nonliving virtual being is now part of our everyday lives.

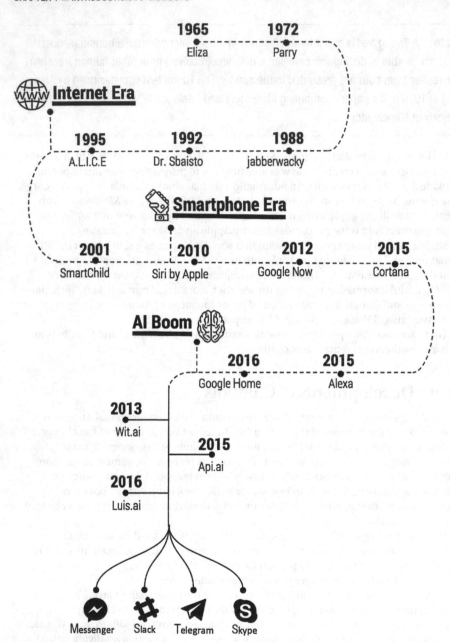

Figure 1-1. Timeline of chatbots

Rise of Chatbots

Chatbots have become quite the buzzword recently, and many people think it is because of the AI hype created by Facebook opening up its Messenger platform for developers to build bots. It might seem like chatbots became a sensation in a very short span of time, but in reality, it is a combination of various factors that occurred from the early 2000s to now.

In this section, we will go through the factors that promoted the recent rise of chatbots and understand how it all makes sense. To give you a sense of where chatbots are headed, quite a few independent researchers are predicting that by the end of 2017, about one-third of the total customer support queries will require some kind of human intervention and the remaining two-thirds will be handled entirely by AI systems.

Growth of Internet Users

The number of people using the Internet in 2000 was 300 million (www.internetworldstats.com/emarketing.htm). This number has grown to 3.7 billion for 2017 (www.internetworldstats.com/emarketing.htm). Internet adoption is growing at 49.6 percent, and as more people get online every day, the power of the Internet grows. Not only has the number of people using Internet gone up, but also the time spent on the Internet by everyone is on the rise. Adults spend close to 28 hours a week on average on the Internet gathering information, talking to friends over social media, or just consuming multimedia content. With the rise in the usage and the number of people, the Internet is estimated to have generated around 1.2 million terabytes of data (1 terabyte is 1,000 gigabytes). The year 2007 marked the emergence of Big Data, which means there is a lot of data that can be mined for information retrieval, and the tools to do so are still being actively developed by large enterprises around the globe. One of the key components for an intelligent chatbot is to have access to data that can be consumed for answering queries posted by users.

For a chatbot to be successful, it needs to be accessed by many people. There are handfuls of platforms on the Internet that can boost such numbers. Facebook saw more than 1.7 billion people use its service in a month and quickly realized the potential for business messaging through chatbots.

Advancement in Technology

All the data that is being generated every day by Internet users will prove to be useless if there are no tools available to leverage the data for learning purposes. In the past few years there has been a boon for the field of machine learning and artificial intelligence. In the early years of 2000s, the machine learning field evolved with addition of *deep learning*, which helps computer machines to "see" and understand things in text, images, audio, or videos. The top technology companies pushed the development of AI to leverage the power of cheap computation to solve hard problems. We witnessed the confidence score of machine learning algorithms go high enough that they can be deployed in a production environment where the experience for real users is enhanced by using these services; this has been made possible because of the availability of large data sets.

The transition of theoretical machine learning problems to practical implementation has helped Internet companies leverage machine learning to grow their businesses. The top technology companies in the world have all contributed in making the machine learning algorithms available in the open for anyone to use and build exciting applications. Google open sourced TensorFlow as a software and cloud service, which was a big milestone in machine learning as it provided the power of machine learning to be leveraged by anyone with a basic understanding of programming. Other companies have pushed in the same direction to make machine learning available to all. For example, Microsoft Azure launched a data/machine learning platform on its cloud offering, and Amazon added machine learning models in its cloud offering, AWS. Netflix started the culture of making developers compete by building models that give better confidence than Netflix algorithms for suggestions of movies. Kaggle took the idea from Netflix and turned itself into a machine learning platform for budding developers to learn from existing large data sets and build powerful inferences.

Developer Ecosystem

In 2003, there were about 670,000 developers in the United States, and that number grew to 1 million developers by 2013. Software engineering jobs have grown at the rate of 50 percent from 2003 to 2013. The developer community is growing at an exponential rate and has been pushing the open source software ecosystem to help develop or improve existing developer tools and frameworks. The advancements and the easy availability of tools and frameworks have led to rapid application development, which is a key component to try new ideas with ease and to fail fast. The API ecosystem has evolved over the last decade, and today it is quite possible to get an API for any application domain, ranging from weather information to critical medical data.

Developers are now able to build chatbots that understand natural language with ease. Once a chatbot understands what the user has said, it fetches the required information by invoking an API or doing a database search. The current developer and API ecosystem is proving to be gold. The developers building chatbots are incentivized to be able to generate revenue to support the development cost, and Facebook, Skype, Slack, web sites, and mobile apps are shaping the platform where developers can deploy their chatbots.

Messaging Platforms

Chatbots came into the limelight because of two players: Facebook and Slack. Because Telegram opened its app for developers to build and deploy bots in June 2015, Facebook announced chatbots on its platform during the F8 developer conference in April 2016, which garnered interest from developers across the globe. All the popular messaging platforms provide developers with a huge consumer base that can be leveraged to provide multiple services via chat.

In this section, we will cover the user interface elements that are used to develop chatbots. Since messaging applications often are accessed on mobile applications, it can be a challenge to develop applications when you are constrained by screen size. One of the hardest tasks developing a mobile application or mobile web site is providing the right information without being too clumsy with the user experience. In fact, 91 percent of the web sites are not optimized for mobile devices, according to a report published by Yahoo. Chatbots solve these issues and add a great value for consumers to access information from various sources via a chat-based interface.

After that, we will briefly introduce features of each of the messaging platforms where you can deploy a chatbot, namely, Facebook Messenger, Skype, Slack, Telegram, Microsoft Teams, and Viber.

Chatbot User Interface Elements

The biggest advantage of using a chat-based interface as compared to mobile/web/ mobile applications is providing the consumer with the ability to convey their intent in natural language as they would speak to their friends. From a developer's standpoint, natural-language text is one of the hardest interfaces to handle. Once a natural-language text request is received, the developer must parse the text into understandable chunks that the chatbot application can understand and then generate a response. It might become difficult at some point in time for the consumer of the chatbot to type each query in natural language; hence, the messaging platforms introduced various user interface elements to make it easy to display certain types of data and enable the user to provide responses to the bot with the touch of a button. In this section, we will go through the most commonly used platform-agnostic user interface elements.

Carousel

A *carousel* is a collection of items that can be browsed horizontally. A carousel contains *cards* that are displayed one by one and that can contain the following:

- Image
- Title
- Subtitle
- Buttons (up to three calls to action, depending on the platform)

7

A carousel layout is used when a lot of data must be presented to the user. The best use cases include showing products (see Figure 1-2), movie catalogs, and so on. The buttons on the card can do two things; either they can send a custom message back to the bot like a specialized command to trigger a flow or the buttons can redirect to a URL.

Figure 1-2. *The carousel layout of a single card on various platforms (Facebook, Skype, Slack)*

Quick Replies

Quick replies are buttons that pop up just above the text box, helping users choose certain options. Quick replies are currently supported only on the Facebook Messenger platform, but you will see how to build a workaround for quick replies for Skype and Slack in Chapters 2 and 3. After the user clicks a quick reply, a developer-defined payload is sent to the bot. Quick replies can contain the following:

- Title

- Text

- Image (optional)

The best use case for quick replies is to prompt the user to make a choice or ask the user for their location (see Figure 1-3). Quick replies are volatile in nature on Messenger because after the user clicks, one of the quick replies disappears. Facebook Messenger allows up to ten quick replies to be shown, and there is a restriction on the length of the title of a quick reply; currently only 20 characters are allowed in the title.

Figure 1-3. *Quick replies on Facebook Messenger*

Buttons

Buttons are key UI elements to help users choose between multiple options (see Figure 1-4). Buttons overcome the length restriction placed on quick replies. Buttons are nonvolatile; in other words, they don't disappear on user tap and can be tapped by the user at a later time. The button action can be one of two types; on user tap, the button can send a developer-defined payload or can open an external URL. The number of buttons that can be displayed depends on the messaging platform, and we will discuss this when we show how to build your first bot in Chapter 2. Buttons can contain the following:

- Title
- Payload text or URL

Figure 1-4. *Buttons on Skype, Slack, and Facebook Messenger*

Web Views

Web views are UI elements that can load an HTML page that might be hosted on your web server. Web views are extensions of the conversational UI to do heavy-lifting tasks that might be too difficult to perform via a chat-based interface. Although web views are currently supported only by Facebook, they are major elements when it comes to the design of chatbots (see Figure 1-5). Web views can be used to display information that is too big to be displayed on the chat interface, such as long answers, or is custom information, such as seat selection. Once the user performs an action on the web view, it is the responsibility of the developer to handle the responses and invoke the right actions for the current user on the back end.

Later in the book, we will introduce how to utilize web views for other platforms that do not support web views out of the box to give the user a richer experience.

Figure 1-5. *Web view on Facebook Messenger*

Feature Comparison

Table 1-1 compares the features of the messaging platforms mentioned in this chapter, as of September 2017.

Table 1-1. *Messaging Platform Feature Comparison*

	Facebook	Skype	Slack	Telegram	Microsoft Teams	Viber
Text Message	✓	✓	✓	✓	✓	✓
Carousel	✓	✓	✓	Partial	✓	✓
Button	✓	✓	✓	✓	✓	✓
Quick reply	✓	✗	✗	✗	✗	✗
Web view	✓	✗	✗	✗	✗	✗
Group chatbot	✓	✗	✓	✓	✗	✗
List	✓	✓	✗	✗	✗	✗
Audio	✓	✓	✗	✓	✓	✓
Video	✓	✓	✗	✓	✗	✓
GIF	✓	✓	✓	✓	✓	✓
Image	✓	✓	✓	✓	✓	✓
Document/file	✓	✓	✗	✓	✓	✓

Summary

In this chapter, you started by exploring the concept of chatbots and learned about their history. We showed a timeline for you to understand the major events that took place in the evolution of chatbots to this date. All the events are incremental, and the success or failure of prior events have led us to the state of technology we have right now. There are many reasons why now is the right time to build chatbots, and we explored some of them, starting from the development and availability of the API ecosystem to the advancements in machine-learning technology.

We also showed you how the user interface elements of chatbots look right now on various platforms. Finally, we provided a comparison chart of the popular platforms (Facebook Messenger, Skype, Slack, Telegram, etc.), which will help you compare the platforms and, depending on your use case, help you choose the right platform to launch your chatbot.

This is just the start. As you read the next chapters, you will get a better sense of how to build chatbots, and by the end of the book, you will have mastered the art of building beautiful chatbots. We are really excited to bring this journey to you.

CHAPTER 2

■ ■ ■

Setting Up the Developer Environment

Setting up the developer environment is half the work.

—Unknown

In the previous chapter, you learned about the significance of chatbots in today's fast-moving world and the history of them. You also looked at the evolution of chatbots through the 1960s up to now. You then looked at various open platforms (Facebook Messenger, Skype, Slack, Kik, etc.) where chatbots can be deployed and how the basic user interface components look.

In this chapter, you will learn how to set up your machine for developing chatbots. By the end of the chapter, you will have a solid understanding of how various components come together, and you will have passed the initial hurdle of getting everything installed on your workstation. We will cover the development setup for Macintosh (Apple), Windows, and Linux machines. We will use open source libraries throughout the chapter, which is good because you don't need to purchase any licenses to get through the chapter.

Let's get started by looking at the framework that you will be using and then move on to installing various software on your workstation.

■ **Note**   We will be using the popular programming language NodeJS to show how to build chatbots. NodeJS is a JavaScript runtime that is built on Chrome's V8 JavaScript engine. NodeJS comes with a large community of open source libraries that are published using Node Package Manager (NPM), which makes working on complex project easier. To get a better understanding of NodeJS, please refer to https://www.nodejs.org.

R. Khan and A. Das, *Build Better Chatbots*, https://doi.org/10.1007/978-1-4842-3111-1_2

Botframework

In Chapter 1, we went through the messaging platforms (Facebook Messenger, Skype, Slack, Kik, Telegram, etc.) that have opened their platform to deploying chatbots. Each platform has its own set of APIs to integrate to be able to receive and send messages. The platforms have adopted similar UI elements. For example, Facebook has cards, whereas Skype has carousels. These are similar UI elements from a user's perspective, but the naming convention is different from a developer's perspective.

There are two ways to proceed further with the book.

- You can choose to build the integration for each platform where you want to deploy your chatbot.

- You can go with an existing solution that already integrates with the messaging platforms.

Building an integration for each of the platforms is complex and time-consuming. Hence, for the rest of the book, we will go with the second option and use Botframework from Microsoft.

Botframework helps connect your chatbot to various platforms with just the click of a button. Botframework does the heavy lifting of integrating to all open messaging platforms (Facebook, Skype, Microsoft Teams, Slack, Kik, etc.) and provides a simple-to-use interface through a NodeJS SDK, C# SDK, and REST APIs to be integrated by your chatbot application. To follow along with this book, you will be using NodeJS as the primary programming language to build your chatbots. We will go through both NodeJS SDK and REST APIs to integrate with Botframework. You will need a Microsoft Live ID to sign up for Botframework services. Please note that the Botframework service is free to use, and you do not need to enter your credit card information.

In the next chapter, we will go through the basics of bot building, including some of the concepts around intents and entities. Also, we will be using Luis.AI, which is already integrated with Botframework, to reduce some of the hassle of building intelligent bots. Luis is an acronym that stands for Language Understanding Intelligent Service; it is a product from Microsoft and is offered as an API for language understanding. Developers integrate to Luis using the REST API provided and then pass each incoming request to Luis, which responds to the chatbot with the intent and entities that were identified. You'll learn more about this in Chapter 3.

Local Installation

Moving forward, you will be developing your chatbot on your local development machine. This will enable you to build the chatbot faster because you can use your favorite text editor and can debug the code easily. Once you have completed the current implementation, you can replicate the setup on a server and have the bot run perpetually. In general, it is always a good practice to build and test locally before pushing the changes to a production environment, so we will follow this methodology here.

As mentioned at the start of the chapter, you will be extensively using NodeJS to build your chatbots. A basic understanding of the following is required:

- Data types in NodeJS (variables, constants, numbers, strings, objects, arrays)

- Flow control (if-else statement, switch statements)

- Loop control (for loop, while loop, for in, foreach)

- Functions

- Promises and callbacks

- How to use NPM to install/uninstall packages

- How to make HTTP requests using the NodeJS/Requests library

- NoSQL database

■ **Note** NoSQL is an approach to storing data persistently where the model of the data does not need to be defined up front. Unlike SQL, where you must create tables and define the relationships between table, you are not required to do the same with NoSQL. NoSQL gives you the flexibility to use any type of data and change the schema of your data without affecting the earlier data. Some of the popular NoSQL databases are MongoDB, Cassandra, CouchDB, and HBase.

Installing NodeJS

NodeJS is a JavaScript runtime, which is predominantly used to build server-side applications. NodeJS has gained popularity in the recent years because of its ability to do tasks asynchronously. It is available for all major platforms and operating systems, and you can download the installer at https://nodejs.org/en/download/.

At the time of writing this book, there are two versions of NodeJS available for download: LTS and current. It is best to download the LTS version, depending on your platform (32/64-bit) and operating system (Macintosh, Windows, and Linux). For this book, we are using LTS version v6.11.2; NodeJS comes with a package manager called NPM that you will use to download Node packages to build your bots. The installation is very straightforward using the installer package that you have downloaded from the NodeJS web site. Run the installer that you have downloaded and follow the prompts (accept the license agreement, click the Next button a couple of times, and accept the default installation settings).

■ **Note** On Windows, you will not be able to use NodeJS until you restart your machine.

Next, you want to make sure that Node and NPM are running without any issues. You can check this by running a few commands using Terminal on Linux and Macintosh (see Figure 2-1) or using the Windows command prompt or PowerShell on Windows machines.

On Linux and Macintosh, open Terminal by finding it in the applications. You can open the Windows command prompt or PowerShell on Windows by searching for them via the Start menu or by right-clicking the Windows icon on the taskbar and typing **cmd**, as shown in Figure 2-2 and Figure 2-3.

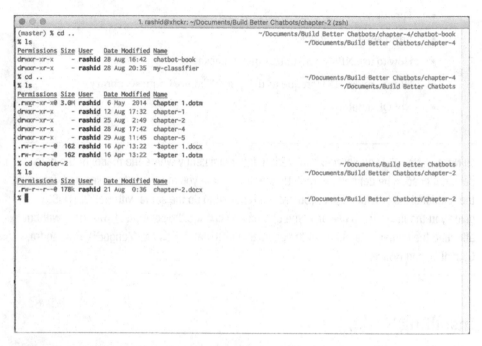

Figure 2-1. *Terminal on Mac and Linux machines*

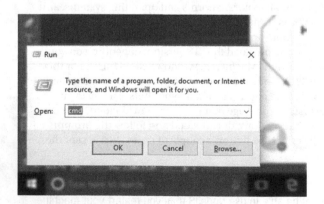

Figure 2-2. *Running the command cmd on Windows to open the command prompt*

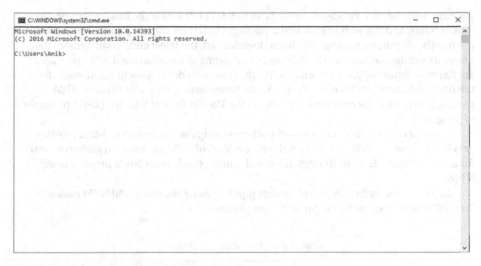

Figure 2-3. *Command prompt on Windows*

Type in the following command to check the Node version:

```
$ node -v
```

This should print the version number of Node that you just installed. For us, it printed the following in Terminal:

```
v6.11.2
```

Similarly, you can check whether NPM was installed properly by checking the version number. In Terminal or a Windows prompt, run the following command:

```
$ npm -v
3.10.10
```

It's fine to have a different version number printed depending on the installation version of your Node and NPM. If you faced an error while executing either of the commands, it might be because of the improper installation of Node. In that case, it's a good idea to uninstall any Node packages and software from your computer and reinstall with the latest Node LTS version.

Following the Development Pipeline

The Node ecosystem is one of the largest developer ecosystems in the world. As a result, hundreds of libraries are available to make a developer's life easier when developing complex applications. The libraries in Node are called *packages*, and packages are managed and distributed through NPM. You can visit https://www.npmjs.com to get more information. Packages can be searched for on the web site by keyword or functionality, and the web site ranks the packages based on various parameters, including the number of times a package has been downloaded, the latest code contribution, the popularity of the package on GitHub, and so on. Some of the most used NPM packages are Express, Browserify, Bower, and Gulp, which are web development frameworks for the back end and the front end. The packages themselves utilize a lot of other NPM packages to reduce the codebase and rely on the Do Not Repeat Yourself (DRY) principle of programming.

On your computer, you can install packages using the npm command-line tool that gets installed with Node. You can set the access level of NPM packages to global or local for a given project. Let's go through the development pipeline for Node projects using NPM.

Figure 2-4 describes the development pipeline using the Node and NPM packages. You will follow this pipeline to publish your chatbots.

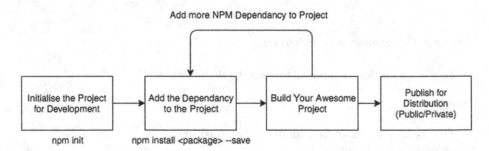

Figure 2-4. *Development pipeline for Node projects using NPM*

You'll now set up your initial project structure and initialize the project that you will be using throughout the book.

Project Setup

It's time to fire up Terminal on Linux and Macintosh (shown in Figure 2-1) and PowerShell or the command prompt (shown in Figure 2-3) on Windows. Navigate to the top-level directory where you want to store the project code. It's always a good practice to have all your projects in an easily accessible location.

```
$ cd path_to_top_level_directory
$ mkdir my-first-chatbot
$ cd my-first-chatbot
$ npm init .
```

Once you run the `npm init` command, the utility will ask you a couple of questions about the project. Depending on your requirements, please feel free to change these values. Figure 2-5 shows the output from running the command on our machine.

```
[1] % npm init .                                                           ~/my-first-chatbot
This utility will walk you through creating a package.json file.
It only covers the most common items, and tries to guess sensible defaults.

See `npm help json` for definitive documentation on these fields
and exactly what they do.

Use `npm install <pkg> --save` afterwards to install a package and
save it as a dependency in the package.json file.

Press ^C at any time to quit.
name: (my-first-chatbot)
version: (1.0.0) 0.0.1
description: Building my first chatbot
entry point: (index.js)
test command:
git repository:
keywords: chatbot
author: Rashid Khan
license: (ISC) UNLICENSED
About to write to /Users/rashid/my-first-chatbot/package.json:

{
  "name": "my-first-chatbot",
  "version": "0.0.1",
  "description": "Building my first chatbot",
  "main": "index.js",
  "scripts": {
    "test": "echo \"Error: no test specified\" && exit 1"
  },
  "keywords": [
    "chatbot"
  ],
  "author": "Rashid Khan",
  "license": "UNLICENSED"
}


Is this ok? (yes) yes
%                                                                          ~/my-first-chatbot
```

Figure 2-5. *NPM sets up the project with initial options and configurations.*

Once the `npm init` command executes successfully, you will see a file named package.json in your project folder. This file contains all the information about your existing project, as well as the dependencies and configuration required to run the project in multiple environments. Let's go ahead and install the packages that are required to build a chatbot. You will need to install the following packages in your project to be able to build a bot that can communicate with other web services.

- `botbuilder`: Botframework provides the Node SDK to build your chatbot and connect to various platforms (Facebook, Skype, Slack, etc.).

- `restify`: Restify is a web service framework for publishing RESTful web services.

- `request`: Request is the HTTP package that helps make web service calls easier.

So, let's open Terminal or PowerShell or a command prompt and install these packages using NPM. Be sure to be in the project directory before executing the following commands:

```
$ cd path_to_your_project
$ npm install --save botbuilder
... Processing & Installing botbuilder
$ npm install --save restify
... Processing & Installing restify
$ npm install --save request
... Processing & Installing restify
```

You have installed the initial packages for building your chatbot. Notice that while installing the packages, you provided an argument --save; this helps you add a package as a dependency to the package.json file for your project. Once you distribute the project or push it to a production environment, you will need all the dependencies to be installed on the server. Let's see how package.json looks now with the added dependencies:

```
$ cat package.json
{
  "name": "my-first-chatbot",
  "version": "0.0.1",
  "description": "Building my first chatbot",
  "main": "index.js",
  "scripts": {
    "test": "echo \"Error: no test specified\" && exit 1"
  },
  "keywords": [
    "chatbot"
  ],
  "author": "Rashid Khan",
  "license": "UNLICENSED",
  "dependencies": {
    "botbuilder": "^3.9.1",
    "request": "^2.81.0",
    "restify": "^5.2.0"
  }
}
```

Storing Messages in Database

Storage is one of the crucial aspects of designing and building a chatbot. The user messages will help you understand the usage pattern of the user by plotting the data and deriving valuable insights. For the scope of the book, you will limit yourself to building a chatbot, so deriving any analytics from the chatbot data would be out of scope. Still, you will employ a NoSQL database to store the messages that are exchanged between the chatbot and users. Specifically, since we are using NodeJS for the bot development, we will employ MongoDB to store all the messages between the user and the chatbot. MongoDB plays very well in the Node ecosystem and comes with a good NPM package to integrate into your application.

While we are using MongoDB to store our data storage, you are free to use any database you are comfortable with. We have chosen MongoDB as the data storage back end because it is simple to set up and provides a good library with NodeJS. The data format used by NodeJS, which is JSON, can be directly stored as it is in MongoDB and can be retrieved and used without involving any external parsers and serializers, which is a big advantage when building applications. This way of storing messages will be the same in all NoSQL databases. Other popular choices for NoSQL databases are CouchDB, Cassandra, and HBase.

In this section of the book, we will show how to install MongoDB on various platforms, define the schema of the message storage, and build out the model API to be used by chatbot engine. MongoDB provides a host of database services that are available as cloud options and as self-hosted. We will be using the MongoDB Community Server, which can be used for free.

Installing MongoDB on Windows

Prior to installing MongoDB, you need to acquire the installation packages. Visit https://www.mongodb.com/download-center#community and choose the Windows tab.

■ **Note** MongoDB works only on 64-bit Windows machines. You might see a couple of versions on the MongoDB download page for Windows. Choose "Microsoft Sever 2008 R2 64 bit and later with SSL" for Windows 7, 8, and newer versions of Windows. For Windows Vista, use "Windows Server 2008 64-bit without SSL."

Once you have downloaded the right installer for your Windows version, you can start the installation process as listed here:

1. Run the .msi file you have downloaded.

2. A set of screens will appear to guide you through the installation process.

3. If you would like to install MongoDB in a customer location, choose Custom in the installation option.

4. You must provide a data directory to store the MongoDB documents. By default, the data directory is the absolute path \data\db.

Now that MongoDB is installed, let's start the database server and connect to the service using the MongoDB client, which comes with the installation. Open your PowerShell or Windows command prompt and type in the following command:

```
# "C:\Program Files\MongoDB\Server\3.4\bin\mongod.exe"
```

■ **Caution**   Windows may pop up a Security Alert dialog box about blocking "some features" of C:\Program Files\MongoDB\Server\3.4\bin\mongod.exe from communicating on networks. Select "Private Networks, such as home or work network" and then click "Allow access."

The previous command should have started the MongoDB server on your Windows machine. Let's now connect to the MongoDB server through the client that is installed by default with the MongoDB server. In your chatbot application, you will need a client built on Node to connect to the MongoDB server. In PowerShell or at your Windows command prompt, run the following command:

```
# "C:\Program Files\MongoDB\Server\3.4\bin\mongo.exe"
```

Installing MongoDB on Linux (Ubuntu)

The MongoDB package is available for 64-bit LTS Ubuntu releases. The packages might work on other Ubuntu releases; however, they are not supported. We will be using the apt package manager on Ubuntu. Let's get started by starting Terminal and typing in the following commands:

```
$ sudo apt-get update
$ sudo apt-get install -y mongodb-org
```

■ **Caution**   Make sure you have root access to the Ubuntu machine where you are trying to install MongoDB. Run both apt commands as root; not having root access will give you an error during installation.

Once the previous commands have executed successfully, MongoDB is successfully installed, as shown printed on your terminal. Let's go ahead and start the MongoDB service.

```
$ sudo service mongod start
```

To verify that the mongod process has started successfully, you can check the contents of the log file at /var/log/mongodb/mongod.log; check for the following line:

```
$ [initandlisten] waiting for connections on port 27017
```

Installing MongoDB on Macintosh

You will be installing MongoDB on Macintosh using the Homebrew package manager. Homebrew is a package manager for the Mac and makes installing most open source software as simple as executing one Terminal command. The best way to install MongoDB on a Mac is using Homebrew, although MongoDB can be installed on the Mac by downloading the binary package from MongoDB's download page. Open Terminal and type in the following commands:

```
$ brew update # Updates all the package information
$ brew install mongodb
$ mkdir -p /data/db # Create the data directory
$ sudo chown -R `id -un` /data/db # Set the proper permissions required by MongoDB
$ mongod # Starts the MongoDB server
```

You can access the MongoDB client by using the following command:

```
$ mongo
```

This will open the interactive shell for MongoDB. You can create a database; delete a database; and add, update, or delete collections for each database. You can execute search queries as well and view the data in your terminal. Let's go ahead and create a test database so that you can add some data and retrieve it. Run the following commands after the MongoDB client is opened in a terminal or command prompt:

```
> show dbs
database_1        0.000GB
database_2        0.000GB
  .
  .
  .
```

The show_db command gives you the list of all the databases that exist in your MongoDB instance. Along with giving the name of the database, it shows the size of each database on your disk in gigabytes (GB).

Let's go ahead and create a new database. This is done by using the mongo command followed by the name of the database. The use command checks whether the database has already been created. If yes, then it fetches the database from the disk and loads it in the MongoDB client so that you can perform a few operations on it. If the database has not been created, the command creates the database and loads it for you in the client. You will create a test database named chatbot-book-db.

```
> use chatbot-book-db
switched to db chatbot-book-db

> db
chatbot-book-db

> db['chatbot-book-db'].insert({'name':'Chatbot book'})
WriteResult({ "nInserted" : 1 })

> db['chatbot-book-db'].find()
{ "_id" : ObjectId("59cb66dce4a56309f6ac3a67"), "name" : "Rashid" }

> db['chatbot-book-db'].insert({'name':'Anik'})
WriteResult({ "nInserted" : 1 })

> db['chatbot-book-db'].find()
{ "_id" : ObjectId("59cb66dce4a56309f6ac3a67"), "name" : "Rashid" }
{ "_id" : ObjectId("59cb691be4a56309f6ac3a68"), "name" : "Anik" }

> db['chatbot-book-db'].find({"name":"Rashid"})
{ "_id" : ObjectId("59cb66dce4a56309f6ac3a67"), "name" : "Rashid" }
```

A new database will not be created unless at least one document is inserted into it. The db variable, which is available to use on the mongo console, refers to the currently loaded databases by the client. You use the JSON notation to select a database and perform some actions such as insert or find. You also apply filters on the find method to filter your search results based on the name. As shown in Figure 2-6, you can even run a command to drop your database. Once a drop operation is performed, all the corresponding data in the database will be deleted and cannot be recovered.

■ **Caution**   Always be careful before running any query on a database because once a query gets executed, the data gets updated as well. Know the implications of running any query beforehand and perform constant backups on data to be able to restore it in the case of an emergency update or delete.

```
● ◯ ◉                                        1. mongo (mongo)
 ✕  mongod (mongod)  ● ⌘1   ✕    mongo (mongo)   ⌘2
% mongo
MongoDB shell version: 3.2.7
connecting to: test
Server has startup warnings:
2017-09-27T14:09:36.664+0530 I STORAGE  [initandlisten]
2017-09-27T14:09:36.664+0530 I STORAGE  [initandlisten] ** WARNING: mongod started without --replSet yet 1 documents are pres
ent in local.system.replset
2017-09-27T14:09:36.664+0530 I STORAGE  [initandlisten] **          Restart with --replSet unless you are doing maintenance a
nd  no other clients are connected.
2017-09-27T14:09:36.664+0530 I STORAGE  [initandlisten] **          The TTL collection monitor will not start because of this
.
2017-09-27T14:09:36.664+0530 I STORAGE  [initandlisten]
> show dbs
botMapping     0.000GB
local          0.000GB
nlp            0.000GB
partyAnimals   0.000GB
test           0.000GB
test-db        0.000GB
vault          0.001GB
> use chatbot-book-db
switched to db chatbot-book-db
> db
chatbot-book-db
> db['chatbot-book-db'].insert({'name':'Rashid'})
WriteResult({ "nInserted" : 1 })
> db['chatbot-book-db'].insert({'name':'Anik'})
WriteResult({ "nInserted" : 1 })
> db['chatbot-book-db'].find()
{ "_id" : ObjectId("59cb6aedb86305ad695fec99"), "name" : "Rashid" }
{ "_id" : ObjectId("59cb6af4b86305ad695fec9a"), "name" : "Anik" }
> db['chatbot-book-db'].find({"name":"Rashid"})
{ "_id" : ObjectId("59cb6aedb86305ad695fec99"), "name" : "Rashid" }
> db.dropDatabase()
{ "dropped" : "chatbot-book-db", "ok" : 1 }
> show dbs
botMapping     0.000GB
local          0.000GB
nlp            0.000GB
partyAnimals   0.000GB
test           0.000GB
test-db        0.000GB
vault          0.001GB
> █
```

Figure 2-6. *Running commands on the Mongo client in Terminal on a Mac*

Summary

In this chapter, you set up your local machine to start building bots. You started off by exploring Botframework and then slowly moved to NodeJS and NPM. Once you had NodeJS and NPM working, you explored the idea of storing messages on your database to perform some analytics later and understand a user's usage patterns. For the storage bit, we went into detail on how to install MongoDB on various platforms and operating systems. You also ran a few queries on the MongoDB client in Terminal or a command prompt to get an understanding of how MongoDB works and how simple it is to query documents.

In the next chapters, you will be using the project structure and modules built in this chapter to enable you to build chatbots.

CHAPTER 3

■ ■ ■

Basics of Bot Building

In this chapter, you'll learn more about how to build your first chatbot and about some design principles. When it comes to the topic of chatbot agents, the important topics are intents, entities, context, and entities. These are the bricks of building your chatbot. In this chapter, you'll learn about each of them and how to use them efficiently.

Intents

Intent is a term used for programmatically identifying the intention of the person who is using the chatbot. A chatbot should be able to perform some action based on the "intent" it detects from the user message. Say you are building a chatbot for a store that sells fashion-related products. Before you start building the chatbot, you need to keep in mind what actions your chatbot will be able to perform. In this case, you would want your chatbot to respond to the user with appropriate textual and visual information when a user wants to see the products that the store sells by saying, for example, "I want to buy a red shirt." Also, when the user sends the chatbot messages such as "Do you have any stores in Berlin?" it should be able to locate all the nearby shops for that particular location. To perform each of these actions, the chatbot needs to decide whether the user is looking for a product or store location from the chat message. So, you can say your chatbot will have two intents: product lookup and location lookup.

Detecting intent from the user message is a well-known machine learning problem. It is done using a technique called *text classification* where the goal of the program is to classify documents/sentences into multiple classes (*intents* in this case). We will show you how you can build a simple classifier using NodeJS later in the book, but for now you will use the LUIS.ai platform that does the heavy lifting for you. Botframework supports a wide variety of languages and SDKs to ease the process of chatbot building. If Botframework does not support or does not have an SDK for your preferred language, it is possible to build a chatbot using the REST APIs provided by Botframework in any language.

© Rashid Khan and Anik Das 2018
R. Khan and A. Das, *Build Better Chatbots*, https://doi.org/10.1007/978-1-4842-3111-1_3

Now head over to LUIS.ai and create your account. LUIS does not require a separate account itself. If you already have a Microsoft account, you can use that to log into LUIS. If you do not have a Microsoft account, you can click the Sign In page on the LUIS home page (Figure 3-1), which will take you to a Microsoft account login page. From there, you can click the "Create a new Microsoft account" link (Figure 3-2). Once you are logged in (Figure 3-3), create a new app by clicking the New App button.

Figure 3-1. *LUIS home page*

Figure 3-2. *Microsoft account login page*

Figure 3-3. *Microsoft account sign-up page*

When you are creating an app, make sure to give it a proper name, as shown in Figure 3-4. This helps you to refer to it easily when you have multiple apps. Once the app is created, you will see multiple things on the page such as intents, entities, and so on. You will learn more about them as you go along with the tutorial in this chapter. For now, let's focus on an intent. As your chatbot will have two intents, let's quickly create your first one. To create a new intent, you have to go to the Intents page by clicking Intents in the left panel. Next, click Add Intent, and you will see the Add Intent dialog pop up.

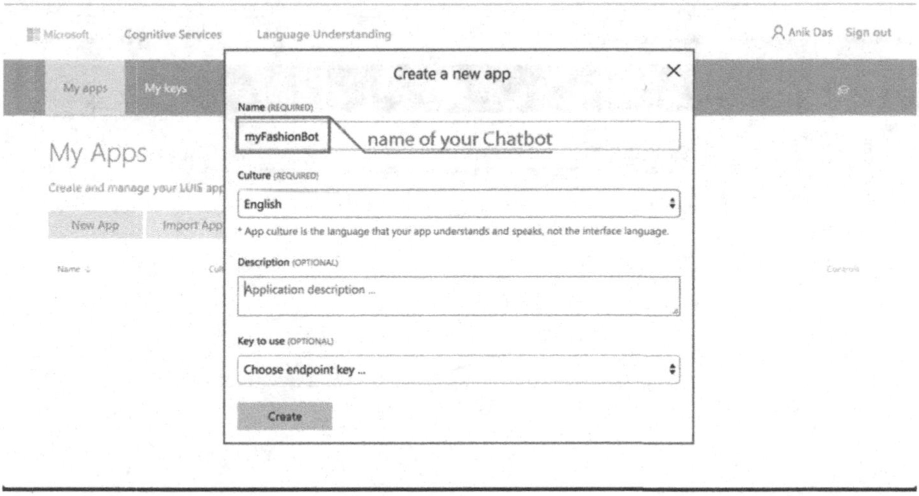

Figure 3-4. *LUIS.ai new app*

Enter the name **product lookup**, as shown in Figure 3-5, and then click Save.

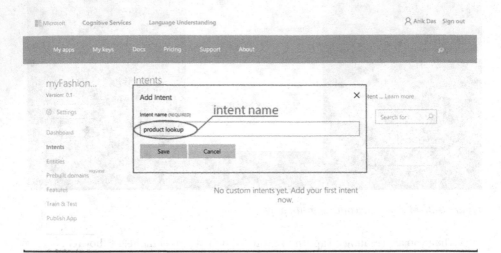

Figure 3-5. *Add Intent dialog*

Once you have created the intent, you will be redirected to the page for that intent. At a first glance, you will notice a few things: utterances, entities in use, suggested utterances, and so on (see Figure 3-6).

Figure 3-6. *Intent home page*

The area of focus at this point is utterances. *Utterances* in each intent are the samples of what user messages may look like for that intent. Go ahead and add the following samples to your Utterances tab for the product lookup intent:

- I want to buy shirts.
- Do you have any gray shorts?
- Show me some red chinos.
- I am looking for formal shirts.
- Can I see some jeans?

■ **Note**   The more utterances/samples you add to each intent, the better the chatbot gets in distinguishing among the intents.

After adding the utterances, click the Save button to save them in the intent. After that, create a second intent called **location lookup** and add the following utterances to the intent:

- Do you have any branches?
- Where are your stores?
- Do you have a store in Berlin?
- Stores near me.
- I want to visit one of your stores.

Save the intent after adding the utterances. Now you have two intents and a few samples in each. To train the model with these two intents, click Train & Test in the left panel, and you will land on the page shown in Figure 3-7.

Figure 3-7. *Training and testing ground of LUIS.ai*

31

Click the Train Application button to train your first model. Behind the scenes, LUIS processes each sample from both the intents and analyzes them. As a result, you get an REST API that you can query with a user message, and it will provide you with the information of which intent the user message belongs to. Using that piece of information, you can easily generate responses for each of those intents. We will cover that later in the chapter.

Once you have trained your model, you can test the model with your own samples to check how the model is performing. Test your model by entering **I want to buy some shirts** in the Interactive Testing section. You will see something like Figure 3-8.

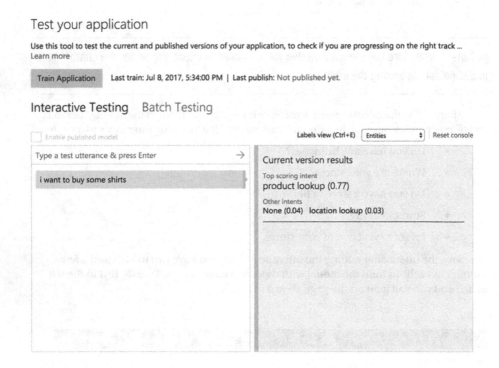

Figure 3-8. *Interactive testing section in LUIS.ai*

You will see that the system is identifying the intent correctly with just a few samples. The number inside the braces of each intent is a confidence score that determines how confident the system is for each intent. You want the score to be as high as possible for desired intent. It's time to publish your first application and start coding your chatbot. Click Publish App in the left panel (see Figure 3-9).

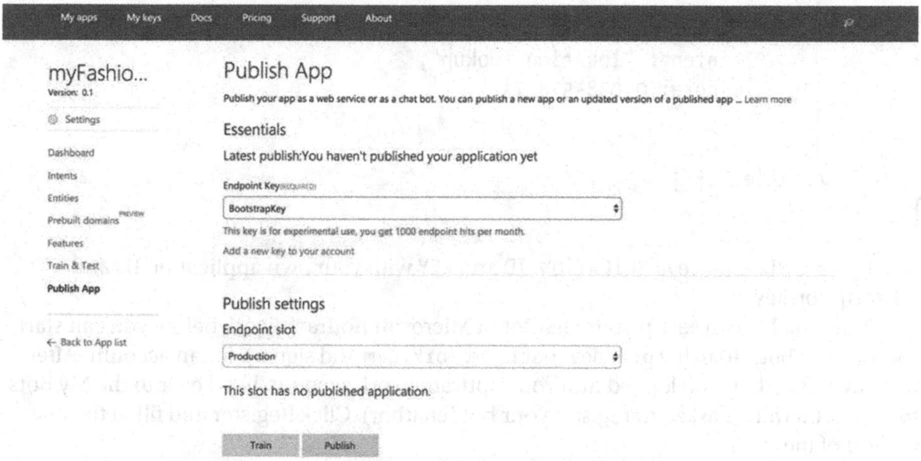

Figure 3-9. Publish app section in LUIS.ai

Select BootstrapKey in the Endpoint Key list and click Publish. Once you have published your application, you will see an endpoint URL similar to this:

```
https://westus.api.cognitive.microsoft.com/luis/v2.0/apps/<APPLICATION_ID>?
subscription-key=<KEY>&verbose=true&timezoneOffset=0&q=
```

(We have replaced our application ID and subscription key with APPLICATION_ID and KEY from the URL.) If you curl the following URL, you will receive a JSON from the API with the detected intent and some other information.

```
url: https://westus.api.cognitive.microsoft.com/luis/v2.0/apps/<APPLICATION_ID>?
subscription-key=<KEY>&verbose=true&timezoneOffset=0&q=i want to buy shirts

response:
{
        query: "i want to buy shirts",
        topScoringIntent: {
                intent: "product lookup",
                score: 0.6905002
        },
        intents: [
        {
```

```
            intent: "product lookup",
            score: 0.6905002
    },
    {
            intent: "None",
            score: 0.0479716361
    },
    {
            intent: "location lookup",
            score: 0.0385578275
    }
    ],
    entities: [ ]
}
```

In the URL, replace APPLICATION_ID and KEY with your own application ID and subscription key.

Now you have to set up your chatbot in Microsoft Botframework before you can start coding your bot. Go to http://dev.botframework.com and sign up for an account. After you have signed up and logged into your Botframework account, head over to the My Bots section. You will be asked to register your bot (chatbot). Click Register and fill in the first section of the form.

If you already have a chatbot created with Microsoft Botframework, you can click the button in the top-right portion of the screen, as shown in Figure 3-10.

Figure 3-10. *Creating a new chatbot (if you already have any)*

Once you click the "Create a bot" button, you will see the page shown in Figure 3-11.

Figure 3-11. *Creating a bot page on Botframework*

Click the Create button, which will pop up a window. From the window, select "Register an existing bot built using Bot Builder SDK" and then click the OK button. Once you click OK, you will be redirected to a page like the one shown in Figure 3-12 with a form to fill in about your chatbot.

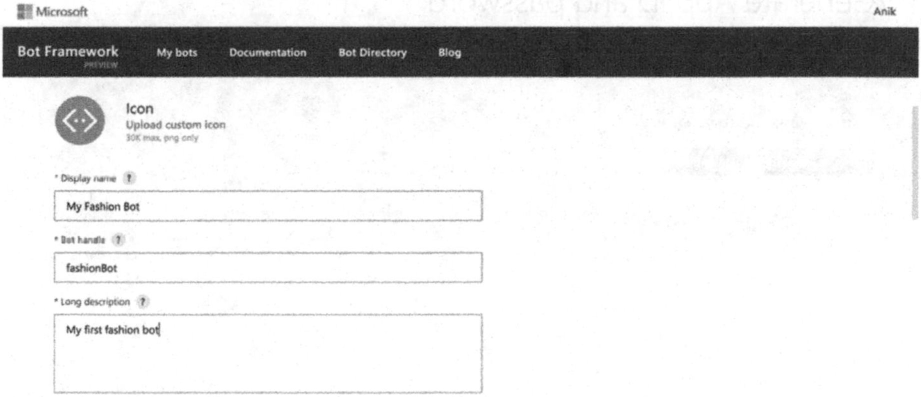

Figure 3-12. *Botframework chatbot registration*

In the Configuration section in the form (Figure 3-13), click "Create Microsoft App ID and password," which will take you to the page shown in Figure 3-14.

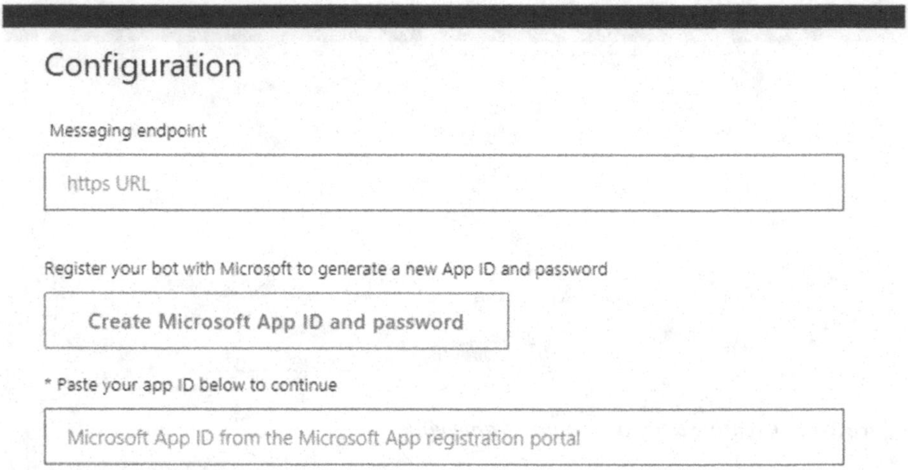
Configuration
Messaging endpoint
https URL
Register your bot with Microsoft to generate a new App ID and password
Create Microsoft App ID and password
* Paste your app ID below to continue
Microsoft App ID from the Microsoft App registration portal

Figure 3-13. *Configuration section in the form*

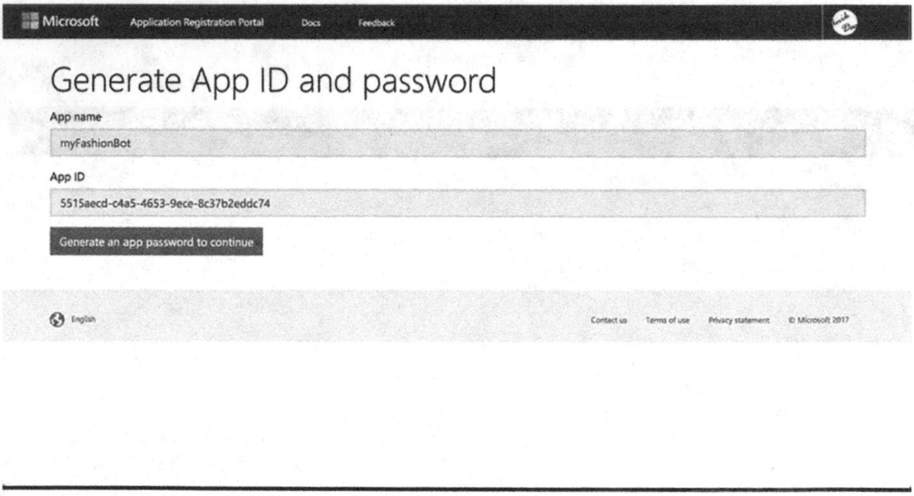
Microsoft
Application Registration Portal
Docs
Feedback
Generate App ID and password
App name
myFashionBot
App ID
5515aecd-c4a5-4653-9ece-8c37b2eddc74
Generate an app password to continue

Figure 3-14. *Application ID generation page*

Copy the app ID from this section and paste it in the Configuration section, as shown in Figure 3-15.

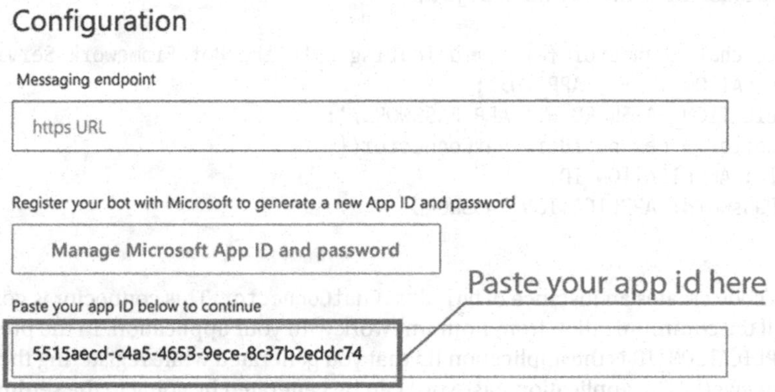

Configuration

Messaging endpoint

```
https URL
```

Register your bot with Microsoft to generate a new App ID and password

```
Manage Microsoft App ID and password
```

Paste your app ID below to continue

Paste your app id here

```
5515aecd-c4a5-4653-9ece-8c37b2eddc74
```

Figure 3-15. Configuration section

Now register your chatbot by clicking the Register button at the bottom of the page.

To understand how the previous code works, you need to understand the underlying technology behind it. The application you are going to develop will be hosted on a server. The server will communicate with Botframework. All your messaging channels such as Facebook Messenger, Skype, and Kik are going to be connected to Botframework. Whenever a user sends a message to your bot on any channel, Botframework will communicate with your application with the message that the user sent. The application will process the message and will send a response. No matter what incoming channel the user uses to message the chatbot, your code will remain the same. That is the beauty of Botframework; it creates an omnichannel communication platform.

To communicate with Botframework RESTfully, you will use a NodeJS module called Restify that enables you to create a RESTful web service in a matter of a few lines. Also, you will use Microsoft's BotBuilder NodeJS SDK to communicate with Botframework.

Let's create a directory called MyFashionChatbot in your computer and create a file called app.js. Inside app.js, you will be writing your logic for the chatbot. Paste the following few lines into app.js:

```
var restify = require('restify');
var builder = require('botbuilder');

// Setup Restify Server
var server = restify.createServer();
server.listen(process.env.port || process.env.PORT || 3978, function () {
    console.log('%s listening to %s', server.name, server.url);
});
```

The first two lines include both `restify` and `botbuilder`. `restify.createServer()` creates an HTTP server instance that you are assigning to your `server` variable. Calling `server.listen()` starts the server, which takes the server port as the first argument and a callback function as the second. The `restify` server is going to run on the port number 3978, but you can choose your own port number for your application. Now append this part of the following code to your `app.js` file:

```
// Create chat connector for communicating with the Bot Framework Service
var APPLICATION_ID = '<APP_ID>';
var APPLICATION_PASSWORD = '<APP_PASSWORD>';
var connector = new builder.ChatConnector({
    appId: APPLICATION_ID,
    appPassword: APPLICATION_PASSWORD
});
```

This code creates an instance of `builder.ChatConnector`. This connector is going to handle all the communication from Botframework with your application. In the previous code, `APPLICATION_ID` is the application ID that you generated while registering the bot in Botframework. The application password can be generated by going to the settings of the bot and then clicking "Manage Microsoft App ID and password" (Figure 3-16). Once you generate the application password, save it somewhere secure as you will not be able to retrieve it again.

Figure 3-16. *Managing your app ID and password on the bot settings page*

Once you have both the application ID and the application password, replace APPLICATION_ID and APPLICATION_PASSWORD with them, respectively. Paste the rest of the following code into your app.js file:

```
// Listen for messages from users
server.post('/api/messages', connector.listen());

// Receive messages from the user and respond by echoing each message back
(prefixed with 'You said:')
var bot = new builder.UniversalBot(connector, function (session) {
    session.send("You said: %s", session.message.text);
});
```

The first argument of server.post, which is /api/message, is the HTTP endpoint path of the application where Botframework will be POSTing the data when a new message arrives. The new builder.UniversalBot statement creates an instance of UniversalBot, which takes your connector as the first argument and a function holding the logic of your bot as the second argument. The previous code implements an echo chatbot; it replies with whatever the user says prefixed with "You said." Notice the session argument passed to the function. It holds all the information about the currently ongoing conversation with the user. For example, you can access the current user message using session.message.text.

You will be testing your chatbot now. Go to Terminal or a command line, navigate to the MyFashionChatbot folder/directory, and then enter node app.js. This will start your RESTful application, which listens to the port number 3978. Next, if you recall from the previous chapter, you have installed a tool called ngrok, which enables you to communicate to your service from the outside world. Open another Terminal window/command line and type in ngrok http 3978. Note that 3978 is the port number you are using in your code. If you are using a different port, replace it with 3978. After running the command, you will see something like Figure 3-17.

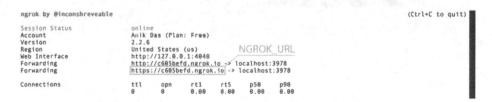

Figure 3-17. Running ngrok instance

Now the local server is accessible from outside through an HTTP link and an HTTPS secure link. Copy the link with the HTTPS prefix, go to the Botframework portal, and open the settings for the chatbot that you have just registered. Scroll down to the configuration part and fill in the "Messaging endpoint" box with `NGROK_URL/api/messages`, where `NGROK_URL` is the URL you just copied (shown in Figure 3-18).

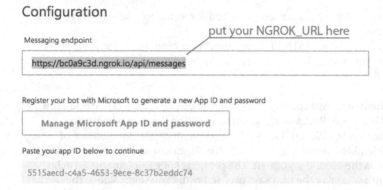

Figure 3-18. *Adding the ngrok URL to the Botframework bot settings*

You are all set. Click the Test button on the top-right corner of the page, and a dialog will pop up. Type **hello world!** and press Enter. Your chatbot will respond instantaneously with "You said: Hello world!" Congratulations! You have made your first chatbot that echoes the user's message, as shown in Figure 3-19.

Figure 3-19. *Testing your chatbot*

Now you are going to integrate your chatbot with the intents that you have just created in LUIS.ai. Your goal is to show all the products available if the product lookup intent is detected and to show a list of all the stores if the store lookup intent is detected. To do that, let's modify your app.js file. Add this function just before where you declared the bot variable:

```
LUIS_APPLICATION_ID = '84e62b56-2c91-478c-b382-320a2985720e';
LUIS_SUBSCRIPTION_KEY = '51ee504e1ac14572b84a07ce9e098dbe';
LUIS_URL = 'https://westus.api.cognitive.microsoft.com/luis/v2.0/
apps/'+LUIS_APPLICATION_ID;
function getIntentFromLuis(text, callback) {
        request.get({
                url: LUIS_URL,
                qs: {
                        'subscription-key': LUIS_SUBSCRIPTION_KEY,
                        'timezoneOffset':0,
                        'verbose':true,
                        'q': text
                },
                json: true
        }, function(error, response, data) {
                if(error) {
                        callback(error);
                }else{
                        callback(null, data);
                }
        });
}
```

This function calls the LUIS web service, retrieves the intent information related to the text that has been passed as the second argument, and calls the function callback when it receives the data from API. You can find your LUIS_APPLICATION_ID and LUIS_SUBSCRIPTION_KEY information on the Publish App tab in the left panel of your LUIS portal. Next, let's modify your bot code as shown next to make use of the getIntentOfLuis function to generate a response based on the identified intent:

```
var bot = new builder.UniversalBot(connector, function (session) {
        getIntentFromLuis(session.message.text, function(error, luisData) {
                var intent = luisData.topScoringIntent.intent;
                if (intent == 'product lookup'){
                        session.send("Sure I will show you all the
                        products!");
                }else if (intent == 'location lookup'){
                        session.send("We have 10 stores across the
                        country");
```

```
            }else{
                    session.send("I did not understand you. I am
                    still learning! Can you rephrase?");
            }
        });
});
```

In the previous code, you are calling the function getIntentFromLuis with the user message as one of the arguments. Based on the intent detected, you are generating a response relevant to that particular intent. Now go to your Botframework account and test your bot. Congratulations, you just have made your first intent-aware AI powered bot (see Figure 3-20)! Now your app.js file should look something like this:

```
var restify = require('restify');
var builder = require('botbuilder');
var request = require('request');

// Setup Restify Server
var server = restify.createServer();
server.listen(3978, function () {
   console.log('%s listening to %s', server.name, server.url);
});

// Create chat connector for communicating with the Bot Framework Service
var APPLICATION_ID = '5515aecd-c4a5-4653-9ece-8c37b2eddc74';
var APPLICATION_PASSWORD = 'bGyKhnsG7gxkQaa6oMxzmvf';
var connector = new builder.ChatConnector({
    appId: APPLICATION_ID,
    appPassword: APPLICATION_PASSWORD
});

// Listen for messages from users
server.post('/api/messages', connector.listen());

LUIS_APPLICATION_ID = '84e62b56-2c91-478c-b382-320a2985720e';
LUIS_SUBSCRIPTION_KEY = '51ee504e1ac14572b84a07ce9e098dbe';
LUIS_URL = 'https://westus.api.cognitive.microsoft.com/luis/v2.0/
apps/'+LUIS_APPLICATION_ID;

// Call LUIS API to get the intent of the user message
function getIntentFromLuis(text, callback) {
        request.get({
                url: LUIS_URL,
                qs: {
                        'subscription-key': LUIS_SUBSCRIPTION_KEY,
                        'timezoneOffset':0,
                        'verbose':true,
                        'q': text
```

```
        },
        json: true
    }, function(error, response, data) {
        if(error) {
            callback(error);
        }else{
            callback(null, data);
        }
    });
}

// Receive messages from the user and respond by echoing each message back
(prefixed with 'You said:')
var bot = new builder.UniversalBot(connector, function (session) {
    getIntentFromLuis(session.message.text, function(error, luisData) {
        var intent = luisData.topScoringIntent.intent;
        if (intent == 'product lookup'){
            session.send("Sure I will show you all the
            products!");
        }else if (intent == 'location lookup'){
            session.send("We have 10 stores across the
            country");
        }else{
            session.send("I did not understand you. I am
            still learning! Can you rephrase?");
        }
    });
});
```

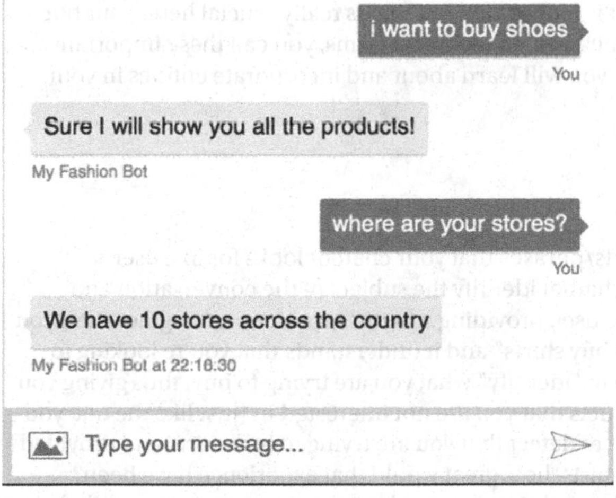

Figure 3-20. *Chatting with your bot*

But there is a little problem. Try sending "Hey" or anything that is out of scope of your bot. The bot randomly chooses one of the intents between product lookup or location lookup or sometimes responds with "I did not understand you. I am still learning! Can you rephrase?" This is not acceptable behavior. Your bot should be confident about what it is replying. To ensure that, you will add a threshold of 0.30 for the score of topScoringIntent. Note that this threshold that you have chosen is based on a completely heuristic method. You can make the threshold higher or lower based on your need, but 0.30 is a good start. Let's modify the bot code to add the threshold.

```
var bot = new builder.UniversalBot(connector, function (session) {
        getIntentFromLuis(session.message.text, function(error, luisData) {
                var intent = luisData.topScoringIntent.intent;
                var score = luisData.topScoringIntent.score;
                if (score > 0.3 && intent != 'None'){
                        if (intent == 'product lookup'){
                                session.send("Sure I will show you all
                                the products!");
                        }else if (intent == 'location lookup'){
                                session.send("We have 10 stores across
                                the country");
                        }
                }else{
                        session.send("I did not understand you. I am
                        still learning! Can you rephrase?");
                }
        });
});
```

Now your bot is pretty confident when it responds for any of the intents. Still, if you look closely, your bot responds generically for all product-related queries. It is not able to identify the product that your user is looking for, but that is really crucial here. Your bot needs to identify the topic of the message. In technical terms, you call these important words *entities*. In the next section, you will learn about and incorporate entities in your chatbot.

Entities

Entities are the important keywords/phrases that your chatbot looks for in a user message. These entities help the chatbot identify the subject of the conversation and deliver targeted information to the user, providing a better experience. Imagine when you message a chatbot with "I want to buy shirts" and it understands that you're looking to buy fashion products but not able to "identify" what you are trying to buy, thus giving you information with all kinds of products that you are not interested in (just like the one you have just developed). If it was able to detect that you are trying to buy shirts and provided you with information only about shirts, how great would that experience have been? You can deliver this kind of experience through your chatbot using a technique called *named entity recognition* (NER), which is a well-known method of extracting important information from text and categorizing it into predefined categories. You are not going to implement NER in this book, but you are going to use the Entities module of LUIS, which takes care of all the technical jargon while you focus on making the user experience richer.

Let's just create these two entities in your chatbot for now:

- Products

- Location

One is a custom entity (product), and the other is a prebuilt entity provided by LUIS.

A custom entity is the type of notion that is exclusively related to your application. You are going to create the products entity from scratch. In addition to being able to create custom entities, LUIS also provides a few system entities that are rather more common knowledge concepts such as location, date/time, dimensions, cardinal, and so on. You are going to use both custom entities and prebuilt entities.

Go to your LUIS portal and click Entities in the left panel. This page contains all the information about the entities that you are going to use in your chatbot. From the Entities page, click the "Add custom entities" button. A modal like the one shown in Figure 3-21 will pop up. Enter **products** and create your first custom entity by clicking Save.

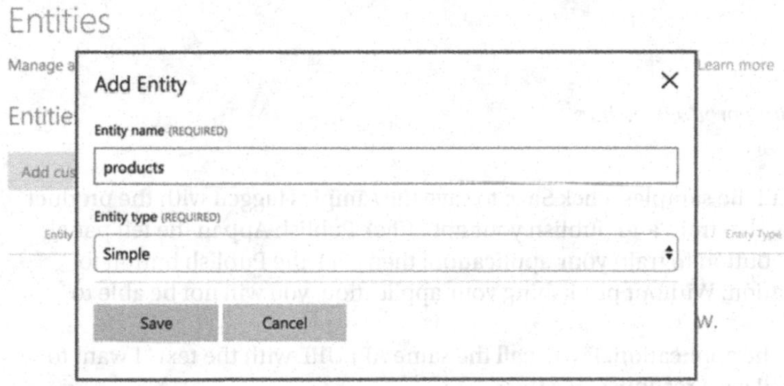

Figure 3-21. *Creating a custom entity*

Now you are going to create your second entity location. Click "Add prebuilt entity" and select geography. Then click Save to create your second entity. After creating these two entities, you need to train your custom entities. Go to the Intents section and open the product lookup intent. Tag all the product names like shirts, shorts, chinos, jeans, and so on, as the product entity, as shown in Figure 3-22.

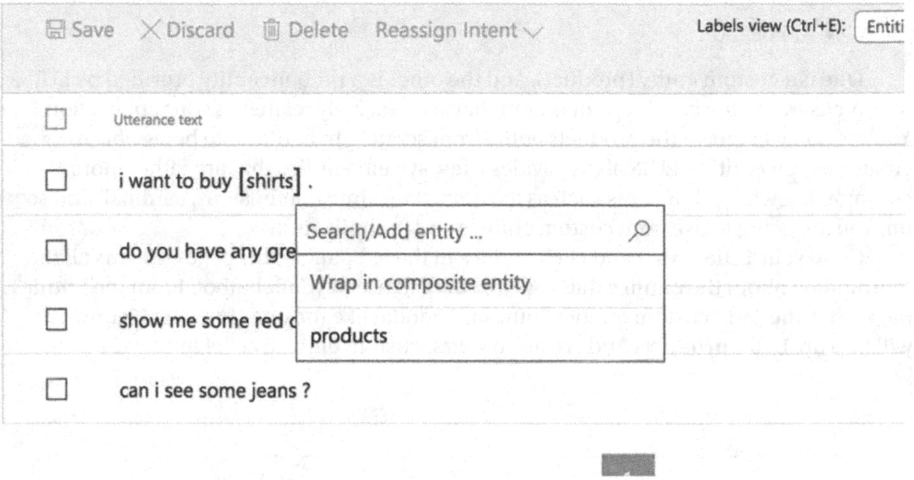

Figure 3-22. *Tagging product entities*

After tagging all the samples, click Save to save the samples tagged with the product entity. Now you need to train and publish your app. Click Publish App in the left panel and click the Train button to train your application; then click the Publish button to publish the application. Without publishing your application, you will not be able to identify entities.

After training the application, if you call the same API URL with the text "I want to buy chinos," you will get a response like this:

```
{
  "query": "i want to buy chinos",
  "topScoringIntent": {
    "intent": "product lookup",
    "score": 0.6903023
  },
  "intents": [
    {
      "intent": "product lookup",
      "score": 0.6903023
    },
```

```
{
    "intent": "None",
    "score": 0.04735379
  },
  {
    "intent": "location lookup",
    "score": 0.0416906923
  }
],
"entities": [
  {
    "entity": "chinos",
    "type": "products",
    "startIndex": 14,
    "endIndex": 19,
    "score": 0.5390309
  }
]
}
```

Similarly, you will get a response as shown here for "Stores in Berlin":

```
{
  "query": "Stores in Berlin",
  "topScoringIntent": {
    "intent": "location lookup",
    "score": 0.956251264
  },
  "intents": [
    {
      "intent": "location lookup",
      "score": 0.956251264
    },
    {
      "intent": "product lookup",
      "score": 0.06805955
    },
    {
      "intent": "None",
      "score": 0.0558308251
    }
  ],
  "entities": [
    {
      "entity": "berlin",
      "type": "builtin.geography.city",
      "startIndex": 10,
      "endIndex": 15,
```

```
        "score": 0.9632844
    }
  ]
}
```

For both these cases, your system is able to detect both the products and location (geography) entity. Let's modify your app.js file such that it detects and makes use of entities while generating responses. Modify the bot code as follows:

```
// Receive messages from the user and respond by echoing each message back
(prefixed with 'You said:')
var bot = new builder.UniversalBot(connector, function (session) {
        getIntentFromLuis(session.message.text, function(error, luisData) {
                var intent = luisData.topScoringIntent.intent;
                var score = luisData.topScoringIntent.score;
                var entities = luisData.entities;
                if (score > 0.3 && intent != 'None'){
                        if (intent == 'product lookup'){
                                if(entities.length > 0){
                                        var products = [];
                                        for (var productIterator in
                                        entities){
                                                products.push(entities
                                                [productIterator].entity);
                                        }
                                        var message = "Sure I will show you
                                        " + products.join(', ');
                                        session.send(message);
                                }else{
                                        session.send("Sure I will show you
                                        all the products!");
                                }
                        }else if (intent == 'location lookup'){
                                // considering only first location
                                if (entities.length > 0){
                                        var location = entities[0].entity;
                                    session.send("We have 10 stores across "
                                    + location);
                                }else{
                                    session.send("We have 50 stores across
                                    the country.");
```

```
                        }
                }
        }else{
                        session.send("I did not understand you. I am
                        still learning! Can you rephrase?");
                }
        });
});
```

You have modified the code in such a way that it will respond to the user based on the product that it has identified for the product lookup intent. For the location lookup intent it will respond based on the location that the user has specified. If the user asks about more than one product, you have joined the products with a comma, thus letting the user know you have knowledge about the subject of the conversation.

You can also try adding a few more entities to the application such as color, size, and so on, to provide the user with an even better experience of information awareness.

Intents and entities are the two basic building blocks of a chatbot. The better the intent and entity detection, the better the experience the chatbot provides. The key to a successful chatbot is to train the intents and entities with ample amounts of samples, with variation in each sample. The variation in samples ensures better generalization of the machine learning model that is working under the hood. In this chapter, you learned and implemented both the key concepts of a chatbot. These concepts will help you grasp the topics we'll cover in the following chapters.

CHAPTER 4

■ ■ ■

Advanced Bot Building

In the previous chapter, you learned about the basic building blocks of a chatbot, including intents and entities. Understanding intents and extracting important entities from the user message are the most crucial parts of building a chatbot. Once you have both of these handled, it's time to present the user with the most intuitive and aesthetically pleasant pinpointed reply.

In this chapter, you will learn how to build a production-ready cross-platform chatbot with the best industry standards and how to build a bot that will interact with third-party API services for getting dynamic information. You will then explore how to store messages that are exchanged between the user and the bot in the MongoDB that you set up earlier in the book. Finally, you will move on to building your own intent classifier based on the naïve Bayes algorithm.

First, in this chapter, we will discuss different UI elements that are available to use on different messaging platforms and how to leverage them to gain a satisfactory user experience (UX).

Design Principles

You all know that chatbots are a new technology altogether. It's like the early age of the Web. Things are still shaky yet growing at the speed of light. That being said, everyone has their own opinion of how to build a chatbot that provides maximum user satisfaction.

Let's say you want to build a new mobile application. The industry of mobile applications is so mature at this point that immediately you probably think of an interface with navigation buttons, tabs, and a canvas full of useful information to interact with. The same goes when you download a new application onto your phone or browse a web site. Once you land on the home screen of the application or the web site, you almost immediately look for few key elements such as navigation buttons, forms, content sections, and so on, which are the elements in most applications/web sites. For the chatbot industry, it is not the same case. There are no specs or guides defined yet that can help you with the development. Yet, it's not impossible to find common ingredients among the chatbots that have been built. The community that has actively been building chatbots do follow some common patterns, which will eventually make it easier for end users to find the common flavor in all the chatbots. We think this will play a major role in democratizing chatbots to the masses. The following are our top suggestions in terms of UX while building a chatbot.

R. Khan and A. Das, *Build Better Chatbots*, https://doi.org/10.1007/978-1-4842-3111-1_4

Keep It Short and Precise

Even though you probably have a lot to convey, do not bombard the user with a big blob of text because they are not going to read it. Keep it as short as possible. If required, break the message into multiple parts and send them in chunks but do not just present a long message. You could also summarize the message and send the summarized message with a button, which will send the detailed message when clicked. For example, this technique works well when you are sending a bill to the user; on the first message, just send the cumulative amount and send a button along with it saying View Detailed Bill. Once the button is clicked, send a nice rich element showing the detailed bill.

Make Use of the Rich Elements

There are a handful number of messaging platforms that you can leverage to deploy your chatbots, and a lot of them support sending rich messages such as carousals, buttons, images, videos, and so on, along with plain-text messages. You can make use of these data-driven rich messaging elements to create an unparalleled user experience. One of the advantages of chatbots is that they can fetch data from numerous data sources such as databases, APIs, and so on, faster than humans and can generate interactive rich messaging elements. For example, a chatbot representing a fashion house will be able to fetch and display a handful of options from the database and present them to the user in a nice carousal with interactive buttons. So, you should use the source-specific rich messaging elements. Later in the section, we will discuss a number of rich elements in detail to give you an overview.

Respect the Source

When a message is sent to the chatbot, it knows the source channel of the message. Sometimes, the source also provides some data about the user, such as name, region, time zone, locale, and so on, that can be made use of. For instance, while greeting the user, you can always start with "Hi, {first_name}." Also, if the locale for the user is available, you can switch the language of the chatbot if the chatbot supports the locale of the user. Moreover, each platform has its own share of messaging options. Facebook Messenger has the widest range of rich message formatting. Slack, Telegram, Skype, Viber, and so on, also have a lot of their own rich message formatting options. It is always good to format the message according to the source. For example, when you are asking the user to choose from a few options or giving them suggestions for what they may say next, you might send a list of buttons for all the messaging channels. If you do that, the experience might vary based on the source. For instance, Facebook Messenger supports sending horizontally scrollable quick replies, which is meant for exactly doing that: giving users suggestions what they may ask or say next. If you keep the source in mind and craft the message based on the origin of the message, it can really enhance the user experience (see Figure 4-1).

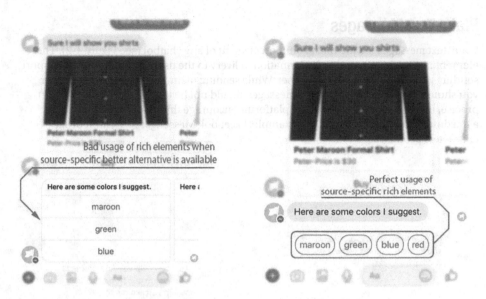

Figure 4-1. Example of usage of source-specific element usage

Use Human Handover

Chatbots are not perfect. We all know that. They are designed to respond to a limited set of queries and make the life of human agents easier. Thus, a chatbot might fail to answer certain queries of the user. Also, a user might get lost in the middle of a conversation. These scenarios happen frequently and can be really frustrating for the end user. Keeping that in mind, it is always smart to use a human failover in certain cases when the chatbot is not able to answer the queries of the user. This will save you from leaving a bad impression of the chatbot by the end user.

Do Not Build a Swiss Army Knife

NLP and AI are not yet able to understand human language like the way you perceive it. So, trying to build a chatbot that does everything will become nothing but a nightmare. Users will get frustrated, and eventually the purpose of building the chatbot is in vein. Try to keep the number of things the chatbot can perform to a minimum if possible. In our experience, when the number of actions that the chatbot can perform exceeds three, it starts to confuse itself when making decisions.

Common Elements

Since different messaging channels have opened up their platforms for developers to create chatbots, they have also introduced numerous UI elements that can be used depending on the situation. We will cover all the common UI elements that are currently available across platforms and then discuss notable elements that are specific to that platform. The following UI elements are available on all the platforms.

Plain-Text Messages

Plain-text messages are the most common element of any chatbot (see Figure 4-2). This element is the primary mode of information delivery to the user. All the platforms support sending plain-text messages to the user. While sending plain-text messages to the user, you should keep in mind that these messages should not be long. They should be short, precise, and to the point. Most of the platforms encourage this, and a lot of them have a maximum message size limit. For example, Facebook Messenger has a limit of 320 characters per message.

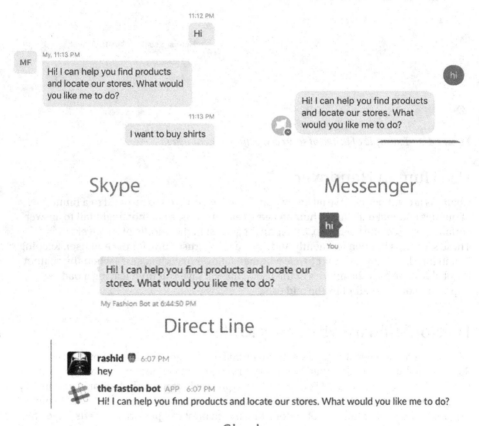

Figure 4-2. *Plain-text messages on different platforms*

Here are some do's:

- Make it short.

- Make it concise.

- Use emojis.

Here are some don'ts:

- Don't send lot of consecutive messages.

Quick Replies

Quick replies are buttons to give the user a hint about what the chatbot may be expecting as a reply to its previous response (see Figure 4-3). Quick replies are great because they give a glimpse of what the chatbot will understand and what it will not. It is a great way to interact with the user when the chatbot is expecting an answer from a subset of information. While quick replies are a great way to interact with the user, it should also be kept in mind that when a user is shown quick replies, it creates an illusion of limited choices. To overcome this, the user can be given an option in the quick reply to input "something else." In general, these quick replies help the user avoid having to type the same message again and again.

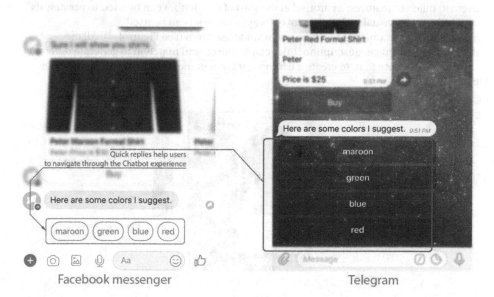

Figure 4-3. *Quick replies in Facebook Messenger*

Here are some do's:

- Make quick reply elements short.

- Definitely use them for getting confirmation.

- Give users an option to manually enter information.

Here are some don'ts:

- Avoid long quick reply messages.

- Avoid long lists of quick replies.

Carousels

Carousels are horizontally scrollable items, with each item containing an image, title, description of the item (optional), and buttons to take user actions (optional). Carousels are great way to showcase similar information in an elegant way, giving the user the flexibility of both viewing the item and taking action on individual items.

To give a few examples, TechCrunch uses carousels to showcase news stories in its chatbot, IFB uses the same thing to view recipes, and so on. You will be using a lot of carousels in your chatbot as well. Carousels are also helpful to showcase a "how to" for the chatbot. Just like every app has an onboarding process where it introduces its users to different features, a carousel at the start of the chatbot can be used to preview its capabilities with visuals. There are lots of ways a carousel can be used.

It's up to your imagination how you want to use them (see Figure 4-4). All the different fields (image, description, title) can be mixed and matched to generate different combinations. Note that, to create a carousel, it is not mandatory to put all the fields in each item.

Figure 4-4. Usage of carousels on different platforms

Here are some do's:

- Can be used to showcase products

- Can be used as an onboarding process

Here are some don'ts:

- Don't send a lot of carousels at once. If more than ten carousels have been sent to user, you need to evaluate the decision-making of the user.

Multimedia Messages

Some chatbot platforms support sending different kinds of multimedia messages such as images, videos, files, and so on. These elements can be used to send images of products, PDFs of bills, and so on, to create a great user experience.

Images

Images, especially GIFs, are really an awesome way to increase engagement with your chatbot. Using little animations, the chatbot can easily convey its messages. GIFs can be used innovatively. A lot of chatbots throw in some GIFs of screen recordings of how to use the chatbot to give an overview. This is a much more interesting way to explain how to use the chatbot than showing some text regarding the usage of chatbots.

Videos

Most of the chatbot platforms allow you to send videos. Even though videos are not popular in the community, nothing beats a stunning video for a product overview. If you are looking for building a chatbot for a product, an introductory video can really help. For instance, when the user asks for the details of a product, a video explaining the different quirks and features can be sent.

Files

A few of the platforms (Facebook Messenger, Viber, and so on) allow you to send certain file types. For sending out receipts in PDF or business-specific files, this can come really handy.

We have mostly covered all the types of UI elements that you are going to use to build your chatbot. Frankly, in most of these cases, these are the elements that you will be using. It also depends on what kind of chatbot you are building. There are no limitations on using different combinations of these elements. We will demonstrate a few of the combinations here in this chapter.

Now let's continue building the chatbot that you started in the previous chapter. Your chatbot has two intents as of now.

- Location lookup

- Product lookup

In most cases, people start a conversation with a greeting, so let's add a greetings intent to your LUIS project. Later you will integrate the greetings intent into your chatbot. The following are the samples you are going to add to your greetings intent. (Intents are the intentions of the user. When a message is received by the chatbot, it maps the message to one of the intents in the scope of the chatbot.)

- Hi

- Hello

- Hola

- Hey

- What's up

- Howdy

- Hlw

You can add as many greetings as you want. You can follow the tutorial in the previous chapter to add an intent to your LUIS application. Next let's train the application to update the machine learning model. After training the model, you have to publish it. You can publish your latest model by navigating to Publish App in the left panel. After you have added the greetings intent to your LUIS application and trained it, you need to integrate the functionality to respond to greetings. In your app.js file, update your bot function like this:

```
var bot = new builder.UniversalBot(connector, function (session) {
    getIntentFromLuis(session.message.text, function(error, luisData) {
        // Intent detected by LUIS
        var intent = luisData.topScoringIntent.intent;
        // Confidence score of the Intent detected
        var score = luisData.topScoringIntent.score;
        // Entities extracted by LUIS
        var entities = luisData.entities;
        // We are setting a threshold of 0.3 for the confidence score
        // If the confidence score is less that 0.3 we are considering that
        // the Chatbot has failed to understand the user message
        if (score > 0.3 && intent != 'None'){
            // Check if the user is looking for any product
            if (intent == 'product lookup'){
                // check if any entities are found
                if(entities.length > 0){
                    var products = [];
                    for (var productIterator in entities){
```

```
            products.push(entities[productIterator].entity);
        }
        var message = "Sure I will show you " + products.join(', ');
        session.send(message);
    }else{
        session.send("Sure I will show you all the products!");
    }
    // Check if the user is looking for location to a store
    }else if (intent == 'location lookup'){
        // considering only first location
        if (entities.length > 0){
            var location = entities[0].entity;
            session.send("We have 10 stores across " + location);
        }else{
            session.send("We have 50 stores across the country.");
        }
        // Check if user has greeted the Chatbot
    } else if (intent == 'greetings') {
        session.send("Hi! I can help you find products and locate
        our stores. What would you like me to do?");
    }
    }else{
        session.send("I did not understand you. I am still learning!
Can you rephrase?");
    }
  });
});
```

Notice that now your chatbot is able to respond to users' greetings. You can test this feature by logging into your Botframework account and sending "hi" to your chatbot. You will receive a message like the one shown in Figure 4-5.

You

Hi! I can help you find products and locate our stores. What would you like me to do?

My Fashion Bot at 21:08:58

Type your message...

Figure 4-5. *One response to greetings*

Showing Product Results

Say you want your chatbot to show some products when a user queries for products. To do that, you need to store some dummy product information that you can search and retrieve. For this chatbot, you will be using a service called Algolia. Algolia is a search-as-a-service product. This allows you to create a robust and powerful search API around your data. For now, you will use the service that we have created. Later in the chapter we will demonstrate how to create your own application on Algolia. So, create a file named search.js in the same directory as your app.js file. This search.js file will contain all the functions to fetch your products from the search API. In that search.js file, create a function named searchByProduct. This function takes an array of product names as an attribute and calls the callback function with an array of search results. This is how your search.js file should look:

```
var request = require('request');

// This function returns products based on the categories
function searchByProduct(categories, callback){

    var options = {
        method: 'POST',
        url: 'http://7m299rv0cn.algolia.net/1/indexes/products/query',
        headers: {
            'x-algolia-application-id': '7M299RVOCN',
            'x-algolia-api-key': '5e3422fe5d9733c5dd8f6da9868f6f5c'
        },
        body: '{ "params": "query=' + categories.join(' ') + '&restrictSearc
        hableAttributes=category" }'
    };

    request(options, function (error, response, body) {
        // Check for any error
        if (error){
            callback(error);
        }else{
            // Parse the text to JSON format
            var bodyJson = JSON.parse(body);
            callback(null, bodyJson.hits);
        }
    });

}
```

```javascript
// This function fetches all the products
function showAllProducts(categories, callback){

    var options = {
        method: 'POST',
        url: 'http://7m299rvOcn.algolia.net/1/indexes/products/query',
        headers: {
            'x-algolia-application-id': '7M299RVOCN',
            'x-algolia-api-key': '5e3422fe5d9733c5dd8f6da9868f6f5c'
        },
        body: '{ "params": "query=&hitsPerPage=10" }'
    };

    request(options, function (error, response, body) {
        // Check for any error
        if (error){
            callback(error);
        }else{
            // Parse the respons to JSON
            var bodyJson = JSON.parse(body);
            callback(null, bodyJson.hits);
        }
    });

}

// Export these functions as modules
module.exports = {
    searchByProduct: searchByProduct,
    showAllProducts: showAllProducts
};
```

You have basically created a module that you can use from any of the other JavaScript files. You are going to use this search module in your app. Whenever you find a product entity in a user query, you will use the function searchByProduct to retrieve the product. It is also possible to create your own function to get product information from any other sources (e.g., databases, APIs, and so on). In this case, you have created a dummy e-commerce store and exposed the search API through Algolia. As the main goal in this book is to purely focus on chatbots, we will not dive deeper into that topic. In the previous function, you are calling the search query API of the Algolia service to search the store inventory for the matching product. Let's integrate the results into your chatbot.

For the ease of understanding, you are going to create a function that sends the product information to the corresponding user. Also, the second function, showAllProducts, fetches the first ten products.

First, you will "require" your search.js file on the top of the app.js file alongside all the other module require statements.

```javascript
var search = require('./search');
```

Then, let's put this function at the bottom of your app.js file:

```
//This function sends the user information about the products in carousels
function sendProductInformation(session, products) {

    // Create a message object
    var message = new builder.Message(session);
    message.attachmentLayout(builder.AttachmentLayout.carousel);
    var cards = [];

    // For each product create a carousel element
    for (var productIterator = 0; productIterator < products.length;
    ++productIterator){
        var product = products[productIterator];

        // Create a carousel element (Knows as HeroCard in Botframework)
        var heroCard = new builder.HeroCard(session);

        // Add product name as the carousel title
        heroCard.title(product.product_name);
        // Add the product brand as the carousel subtitle
        heroCard.subtitle(product.brand);
        // Use the carousel text element for showing price
        heroCard.text("Price is " + product.price);
        // Add product image to the carousel by creating CardImage Object
        with the image URL
        heroCard.images([builder.CardImage.create(session, product.image)]);
        heroCard.buttons([builder.CardAction.imBack(session, "i want to buy
        " + product.category, "Buy")]);

        cards.push(heroCard);
    }

    message.attachments(cards);
    session.send(message);

}
```

The previous function takes the user session and products as arguments and sends product information to the user. The function session.send takes a message object as an input. This message object can be a plain-text message or a rich UI message such as a carousel, buttons, or more. In this case, you are sending a list of HeroCard elements, which are basically carousels. Now let's explain the function line by line.

```
var message = new builder.Message(session);
message.attachmentLayout(builder.AttachmentLayout.carousel);
```

In the first line, you are telling the builder to create an empty message and to store it in the message variable. In the next line, you are setting the message layout to the carousel by explicitly stating that as an argument to the message.attachmentLayout function. At this point, it may seem a little difficult to understand, but trust me that you are going to use them a lot and eventually get used to them. Now let's look at the for loop.

In the for loop, you are creating each HeroCard element like this:

```
var heroCard = new builder.HeroCard(session);
heroCard.title(product.product_name);
heroCard.subtitle(product.brand);
heroCard.text("Price is " + product.price);
heroCard.images([builder.CardImage.create(session, product.image)]);
heroCard.buttons([builder.CardAction.imBack(session, "i want to buy " +
product.category, "Buy")]);
```

Calling new builder.HeroCard(session) creates an instance of an empty HeroCard element. You need to populate the instance with related information. In the following lines, you are populating the HeroCard element with the title, the subtitle, text, an image, and a button. The interesting thing here is creating the button. On each card you will put one button for now. It is a best practice to use no more than three buttons per card. With the increasing number of buttons, it raises the confusion level, and there is a cross-platform compatibility issue as well. Facebook Messenger does not allow you to add more than three buttons per carousel element. In this chatbot, you will stick to three buttons per card as well. Now Botframework supports creating different kinds of buttons. For now, you are going to use builder.CardAction.imBack buttons. Notice the arguments of the builder.CardAction.imBack constructor. The second argument is basically a string that is going to be sent as a text message, and the third argument is the title of the button.

```
message.attachments(cards);
session.send(message);
```

In the previous lines, you are attaching the cards to your message and sending them to the user. Now change the bot function in your app.js file where the product lookup intent is handled like this:

```
if (intent == 'product lookup'){
    if(entities.length > 0){
        var products = [];
        for (var productIterator in entities){
            products.push(entities[productIterator].entity);
        }

        session.send("Sure I will show you " + products.join(', '));
        search.searchByProduct(products, function (error, productResult) {
            sendProductInformation(session, productResult);
        });
    }else{
        session.send("Sure I will show you all the products!");
```

```
    search.showAllProducts(products, function (error, productResult) {
        sendProductInformation(session, productResult);
    });
  }
}
```

Whenever the product lookup intent is detected, you are checking whether a corresponding entity is detected. If an entity is found, you send a message acknowledging the fact that you have understood the user intention, and then you fetch the related product using your search module function searchByProduct. When you are unable to find a product to search for (aka when no entities are found in the user query), you still show the user ten products from your inventory (see Figure 4-6). Now let's test your chatbot.

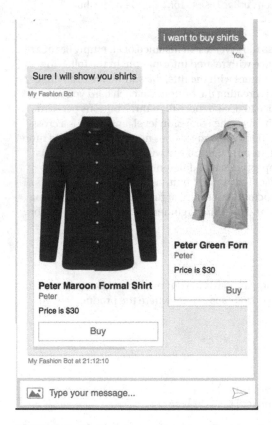

Figure 4-6. *Chatbot responding to product queries*

Your chatbot now has some intelligence and integration with your system. It's still lacking one major important topic; it's not able to retain information about any user. As you are building a fashion chatbot, people will be filtering the products by color. Now you will add the functionality to your chatbot so that it can remember what product and color the user has searched for. Basically, you are going to have your chatbot to retain context-aware information.

Let's make your chatbot remember what product your user has searched for. To do that, you will use Botframework's built-in features. Botframework allows you to store conversation-specific data. In your app.js file, let's add this code right before where you are calling your search function searchByProduct.

```
session.conversationData.products = products;
session.save();
```

Now Botframework will remember what product the user has searched for. Next, you are going to give the user flexibility to filter the results with their color preference, keeping the product in context. Let's quickly create a color filter intent and a color entity in your LUIS application. Then let's add the following samples to your color filter intent, tagging the color entity in each of them.

- I want in black.

- Show me something in red.

- Do you have this in green?

- Filter them by blue.

- I prefer grey.

- Can I get this in maroon?

Once you are done adding the samples to your intent, you are going to train and publish your LUIS application, thus making the new intent available to your application. Next, let's integrate the functionality to address the new intent. Add this new function to your search.js file:

```
function searchByProductFilterByColor(categories, colors, callback){

    for (var i=0; i< colors.length; ++i){
        colors[i] = 'color:'+colors[i]
    }

    var filterQuery = colors.join(' OR ');

    var options = {
        method: 'POST',
        url: 'http://7m299rv0cn.algolia.net/1/indexes/products/query',
        headers: {
            'x-algolia-application-id': '7M299RV0CN',
            'x-algolia-api-key': '5e3422fe5d9733c5dd8f6da9868f6f5c'
        },
        body: '{ "params": "query=' + categories.join(' ') + '&filters='+
filterQuery +'&restrictSearchableAttributes=category" }'
    };
```

```
request(options, function (error, response, body) {
    if (error){
        callback(error);
    }else{
        var bodyJson = JSON.parse(body);
        callback(null, bodyJson.hits);
    }
});

}
```

You also have to add this function to the module, as shown here:

```
module.exports = {
    ...
    searchByProductFilterByColor:searchByProductFilterByColor
};
```

Let's change your bot function in the app.js file as well to handle the color filter intent.

```
...
} else if (intent == 'greetings') {
    session.send("Hi! I can help you find products and locateour stores.
What would you like me to do?");
} else if (intent == 'color filter') {

    var colors = [];
    for (var colorIterator in entities){
        if (entities[colorIterator].type == 'color'){
            colors.push(entities[colorIterator].entity);
        }
    }
    var productsFromContext = session.conversationData.products;

    session.send("Sure I will show you " +
        productsFromContext.join(', ') +
        ' in ' +
        colors.join(' '));

    search.searchByProductFilterByColor(
        productsFromContext,
        colors,
        function (error, productResult) {
            sendProductInformation(session, productResult);
        }
    );
}
...
```

In the previous code, you are basically looking for the color entity when the intent is detected. Then you search through your catalog of products via the search API you integrated in the searchByProductFilterByColor function in search module. Let's go and test your chatbot with the context integrated.

Now that your chatbot is able to understand product-related queries and is able to filter the result by color, you can add a little more smartness to it. When the list of product is shown, you can also suggest some colors to your user (see Figure 4-7). But there is a catch here: out of the box, Botframework does not allow you to send buttons. So, you are going to make use of the HeroCard element without the image to send these color suggestions. But these buttons will not load on some platforms, thus breaking the user experience on some platforms. To avoid that, you can send platform-specific payloads. For example, Facebook Messenger allows you to send beautiful quick replies, instead of sending HeroCard elements. For Facebook Messenger, you are going to send quick replies.

Figure 4-7. *Chatbot replying to color-related queries*

First, you will add the functionality to send color suggestions to the user. To do that, let's write a function called sendColorSuggestion like this:

```
function sendColorSuggestion(session, products){
    var colors = [];

    for (var productIterator = 0; productIterator < products.length;
    ++productIterator) {
        var product = products[productIterator];
        if (colors.indexOf(color) == -1){
            colors.push(product.color);
        }
    }

    var message = new builder.Message(session);
    message.attachmentLayout(builder.AttachmentLayout.carousel);

    var heroCard = new builder.HeroCard(session);
    var buttons = [];

    for (var colorIteraror = 0; colorIteraror < colors.length; ++colorIteraror) {
        var color = colors[colorIteraror];

        // To make sure the buttons are not duplicated
        var button_text = "Do you have this in " + color;
        var button = builder.CardAction.imBack(session, button_text, color);

        buttons.push(button);

    }

    heroCard.title('Here are some colors I suggest.');
    heroCard.buttons(buttons);

    message.attachments([heroCard]);
    session.send(message);

}
```

The previous function takes the session and products arrays as arguments and creates a new array called colors from the products array and then sends a HeroCard element only with the title and buttons in it. Let's call this function when the product lookup intent is triggered.

```
search.searchByProduct(products, function (error, productResult) {
    sendProductInformation(session, productResult);
    sendColorSuggestion(session, productResult);
});
```

Let's add the Facebook Messenger-specific payload to send quick replies. You will create another function called sendColorSuggestionFB, which you will use to send the color suggestion quick replies to Facebook Messenger users.

```
function sendColorSuggestionFB(session, products){
    var colors = [];

    for (var productIterator = 0; productIterator < products.length;
    ++productIterator) {
        var product = products[productIterator];
        colors.push(product.color);
    }

    var message = new builder.Message(session);
    var quicReplies = [];

    // Limit the maximum number of quick replies to 10 (10 is the limit set
    by messenger
    for (var colorIteraror = 0; colorIteraror < 10 && colorIterator
    < colors.length; ++colorIteraror) {
        var color = colors[colorIteraror];

        var quickReply = {
            "content_type":"text",
            "title": color,
            "payload":"do you have this in " + color
        }
        quicReplies.push(quickReply)

    }

    message.sourceEvent({
        facebook: {
            text: 'Here are some colors I suggest.',
            quick_replies: quicReplies
        }
    })

    session.send(message);
}
```

Also, you have to change your chatbot logic to check for the source facebook and send quick replies accordingly. The source of the message can be accessed as session. message.source. Let's change the chatbot logic as follows:

```
...
search.searchByProduct(products, function (error, productResult) {
    sendProductInformation(session, productResult);

    if (session.message.source == 'facebook'){
        sendColorSuggestionFB(session, productResult);
    }else{
        sendColorSuggestion(session, productResult);
    }
});
...
```

Let's dive deep into the code. If the source is facebook, you are going to call the function sendColorSuggestionFB with the session associated and the productResult array. Inside the function you construct the quickReplies array by following the Facebook Messenger platform documentation. An example quick reply object looks like the following:

```
{
    "content_type":"text",
    "title":"Search",
    "payload":"<POSTBACK_PAYLOAD>",
    "image_url":"http://example.com/img/red.png"
}
```

The title is what will be visible to the user on the button. When the button is clicked, you will receive the playload as a postback. So, for each of your color quick reply buttons, you set the quick reply payload to be "Do you have this in <color>?" Whenever the user clicks one of the quick replies, you get this payload as a normal text message. Now we'll explain how to send this custom object to Facebook users. Botframework allows you to send custom platform-specific data when you are sending a message. You can do that using the message.sourceEvent function. This function allows you to set a custom object for specific platform in a specific format, as shown here:

```
{
    facebook: {
        ...
    }
}
```

As shown previously, you can send a custom payload to enhance the UX for individual platforms. We highly recommend playing around with this functionality to provide users with the best user experience for your chatbot (see Figure 4-8, Figure 4-9, and Figure 4-10).

Figure 4-8. *Chatbot providing color suggestions*

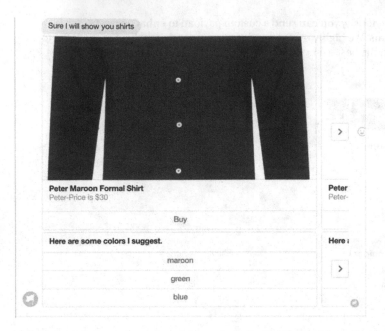

Figure 4-9. *Color suggestion on Messenger before adding quick replies through sourceEvent*

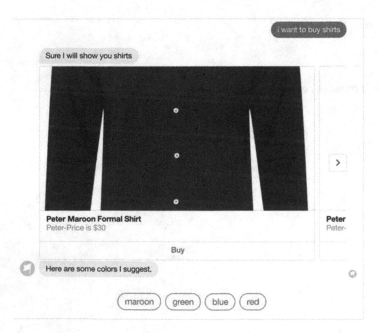

Figure 4-10. *Color suggestion on Messenger after adding quick replies*

Integrating Location Lookup Intent

You are done integrating the product intent. Now you will integrate the location lookup intent that you created in the previous chapter with the store location data you have available. We have already created an API that allows you to look up stores available in a city. You are going to use that API to fetch the store your user is looking for and send the information. Again, this is just a demo API; you can always hook up your own data source such as from any database or API to your chatbot. As usual, you will create a search function in your search.js file to look up.

```
function searchStoreByCity(cities, callback){

    var options = {
        method: 'POST',
        url: 'http://7m299rv0cn.algolia.net/1/indexes/store_locations/query',
        headers: {
            'x-algolia-application-id': '7M299RVOCN',
            'x-algolia-api-key': '5e3422fe5d9733c5dd8f6da9868f6f5c'
        },
        body: '{ "params": "query=' + cities.join(' ') + '&restrictSearchabl
        eAttributes=city" }'
    };

    request(options, function (error, response, body) {
        if (error){
            callback(error);
        }else{
            var bodyJson = JSON.parse(body);
            callback(null, bodyJson.hits);
        }
    });

}
```

The API returns an array of objects that correspond to the locations of stores in a city. Also, let's add this function to the module with the rest of the functions.

```
module.exports = {
    ...
    searchStoreByCity:searchStoreByCity
};
```

In this way, your function searchStoreByCity will be accessible to all the other modules in your application. Let's call the function whenever the location lookup intent is triggered and a location entity is found. Now you will make changes to your chatbot logic in the app.js file. Let's create a function that takes a list of city entities found in the user query, calls your API, and then sends a list of HeroCard elements to the respective user.

```javascript
function sendStoreList(session, cities){

    var message = new builder.Message(session);
    message.attachmentLayout(builder.AttachmentLayout.carousel);
    var cards = [];

    search.searchStoreByCity(cities, function(err, stores) {
        if (stores.length > 0){
            session.send('Sure we have got stores in '+ cities.join(', '));
            for (var storeIterator=0; storeIterator < stores.length;
            ++storeIterator){

                var store = stores[storeIterator];

                var heroCard = new builder.HeroCard(session);

                heroCard.title(store.city);
                heroCard.text(store.street);

                cards.push(heroCard);
            }

            message.attachments(cards);
            session.send(message);

        }else{
            session.send('Sorry we do not have any stores in '+ cities.
            join(', '));
        }
    });

}
```

The previous function is pretty straightforward. It takes the current user session and a list of cities as arguments, constructs HeroCard elements for each location with details of the stores (street address and city name), and sends them back to the user.

In Figure 4-11, the chatbot is replying to the user with the relevant information about the different store locations of the business.

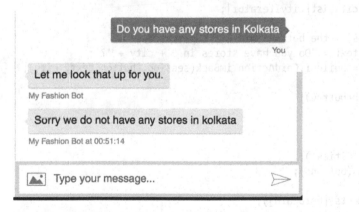

Figure 4-11. *Chatbot responding to store location–related queries*

In Figure 4-12, you can see that if there are no stores are found for the requested location by the user, the chatbot gracefully falls back with an apologetic tone.

Figure 4-12. *Chatbot responding to no stores found*

Next, you will add another function called sendCitySuggestions that sends a list of most popular cities with the most popular stores. With this functionality, even if your chatbot is not able to identify the city the user is searching for a store in, you can still give them an option to browse through the list of popular cities. Let's implement the following function:

```
function sendCitySuggestions(session) {
    session.send('No city found in your query to look up our stores! But
    these are the cities where our stores are most popular.');

    var cityList = [
        "London",
        "Bangkok",
        "Singapore",
        "New York",
        "Kuala Lumpur",
        "Hong Kong",
        "Dubai"
    ]

    var message = new builder.Message(session);
    message.attachmentLayout(builder.AttachmentLayout.carousel);

    var heroCard = new builder.HeroCard(session);
    var buttons = [];

    for (var cityIterator = 0; cityIterator < cityList.length;
    ++cityIterator) {
        var city = cityList[cityIterator];

        // To make sure the buttons are not duplicated
        var button_text = "Do you have stores in " + city + '?';
        var button = builder.CardAction.imBack(session, button_text, city);

        buttons.push(button);

    }

    heroCard.title('Cities');
    heroCard.buttons(buttons);

    message.attachments([heroCard]);
    session.send(message);

}
```

Great, now you have all the tools to handle the user queries for the location lookup. Change the chatbot logic for the location lookup intent as follows:

```
...
if (intent == 'location lookup') {
    // considering only first location
    var cities = [];

    if (entities.length > 0) {
        for (var locationIterator = 0; locationIterator < entities.length;
        ++locationIterator) {
            var entityObject = entities[locationIterator];
            if (entityObject.type == 'builtin.geography.city') {
                cities.push(entityObject.entity);
            }
        }
    }

    if (cities.length > 0) {
        session.send('Let me look that up for you.')
        sendStoreList(session, cities);
    } else {
        sendCitySuggestions(session);
    }
}
...
```

With this, you are done with implementing your first smart end-to-end chatbot that can show product suggestions with context management and can also provide information about stores available in a particular city. Feel free to get your hands dirty with all the features that cannot be covered in this book's pages. Chatbots have endless potential to disrupt a lot of existing solutions because of recent innovations, great user experiences, accessibility, ease of use, and many other features (see Figure 4-13). So, without further ado, let's start writing your first chatbot.

■ **Tip**   You can use quick replies to send the list of cities for a better user experience on selective platforms.

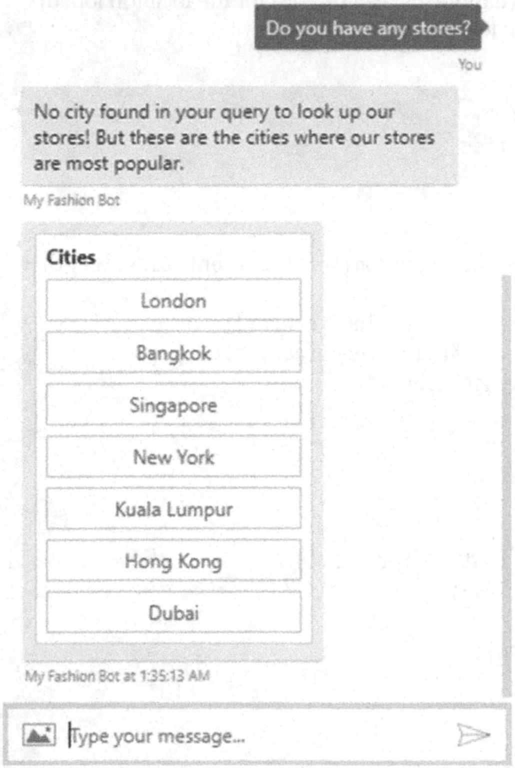

Figure 4-13. *Chatbot giving store suggestions*

There are few caveats in your implementation of this chatbot. We will mention them in brief, you should try to fix them yourself, which will help you gain a deeper understanding of how everything works.

Saving Messages

You built a full-blown chatbot in the previous section, which is not just a button-based bot but is a full-blown chatbot that understands natural language. It provides the user with the freedom to type what is on their mind without worrying too much. You also launched the chatbot on various channels and saw how each channel's UX/UI patterns came in handy when designing your chatbot. One of the most important aspects of a fully implemented chatbot is the analytics it provides. You will learn in greater detail what the basic metrics are that you should track for a production-level bot in Chapter 5.

In this section, you will set up the basic architecture for saving the messages in a persistent database. Remember that you installed MongoDB in Chapter 2? Well, you are going to use your MongoDB instance and store the messages that are sent by the user and the messages that are sent by the bot in response. Once you store all the interactions between the user and the chatbot, you can then plug the analytics into a UI module and visualize the data. For the scope of the chatbot in this book, you will restrict yourself to just storing the data. In the code, which will be on GitHub, you will add the API to export the data in a JSON format that can then be consumed by your UI application for visualization.

■ **Note** We have used MongoDB for the messages store in this book, but you are free to use the database of your choice. Our choice was based on the ease of setup and compatibility with Node.

Getting Mongoose

MongoDB is a stand-alone NoSQL database that has a lot of ODM developed by open source enthusiasts. To connect the example bot application's back end to MongoDB, we will show how to use Mongoose ODM, which was released by the good folks Automattic (the company behind WordPress). Let's go ahead and install Mongoose in your application.

```
$ cd <path_to_your_application>
$ npm install --save mongoose
```

You can install Mongoose using the NPM module, which we discussed in Chapter 2. The dependency is added to your package.json file, which will be helpful when you push your bot to production.

Building the Message Model

MongoDB is a document-oriented database, which gives you the flexibility to store any JavaScript object as it is in the database. Mongoose provides a well-defined API to search for the stored data with the ability to apply filters. Let's go ahead and define the fields that you will need to store in the database.

- *Source*: The source of the message (Facebook, Slack, Skype, etc.)

- *From*: Who sent the message (the unique ID of the person/bot)

- *To*: To whom the message was sent (the unique ID of the person/ bot)

- *Payload*: The payload that was received from the incoming/ outgoing message to examine the type of message and the attachments

- *Creation Time*: The ability to understand patterns when users are interacting with the chatbot

Adding the Model File

It is a best practice to modularize the code in multiple files, with each file handling only one broad functionality. As you did when creating search.js, go ahead and create a mode.js file in your favorite text editor in the root directory of your project. The first thing you will need to do is import the Mongoose module, which you installed in the previous section, and configure it to use your local installation of the MongoDB database.

Model.js file
```
var mongoose = require ('mongoose');
var schema = mongoose.Schema;
mongoose.connect ('mongodb://localhost:27017/DB_NAME');
```

Now your application can connect to the MongoDB database using the Mongoose ODM. In the place of DB_NAME, provide any name for the database. Make sure the database name provided is already created using the Mongo client on the command line. Let's now define your message schema, which you will be storing as collections in the MongoDB database. (Each object in the database is called a *collection* in MongoDB.) Add the following code in the mode.js file after the previous connection handling:

```
var BOT_NAME = 'shop_assistant';
var messageSchema = new mongoose.Schema({
        from: String,
        to: String,
        createdTime: Date,
        source: String,
        payloadObject: schema.Types.Mixed
)};
```

You will notice you have created a new object instance of the Schema type and have told Mongoose how your collection object will look. It is good practice to tell Mongoose in advance about the type of variable you will be storing; it also helps other developers reading your code to understand what each field stores in the collection. The Mixed type of schema basically tells Mongoose that you are going to store a JavaScript object (JSON) in the field. String and Date are the primitive JavaScript types that are provided out of the box by the Node environment. Now let's go ahead and define your message model for Mongoose.

```
var messageModel = mongoose.model ('Messages', messageSchema);
```

The schema and model are defined, which are interlinked. Now let's define two functions that will be exported to app.js. The first function is saveSentMessage, which will be invoked when the bot responds to the user query. The saveSentMessage function takes one argument, which is named payload. This is the object generated by Botbuilder. The second function is saveIncomingMessage, which is invoked whenever the user messages the bot; saveIncomingMessage also takes one argument called payload, which is provided by Botbuilder.

```
function saveSentMessage (payload) {
        var sentmessage = new messageModel ({
                from: BOT_NAME,
                to: payload.address.user.id,
                createdTime: new Date(),
                source: payload.source,
                payloadObject: payload
        });
        sentMessage.save (function(err){
                if (err) {
                        console.log (`Error saving message: Message to
                        ${payload.user.id}`);
                } else {
                        console.log (`Message saved successfully`);
                }
        });
}
```

You have hard-coded the BOT_NAME variable at the top of the file. This will help you to query the database easily based on the BOT_NAME in the To or From field. Let's add the implementation of the saveIncomingMessage function.

```
function saveIncomingMessage (payload) {
        var incomingMessage = new messageModel ({
                from: payload.address.user.id,
                to: BOT_NAME,
                createdTime: new Date(),
                source: payload.source,
                payloadObject: payload
        });
        incomingMessage.save(function (err) {
                if (err) {
                        console.log (`Error saving message: Message from
                        ${payloaod.user.id}`);
                } else {
                        console.log (`Message saved successfully`);
                }
        });
}
```

You have implemented your model, and now you need to export the two functions that can be consumed by app.js.

```
module.exports = {
        saveSentMessage: saveSentMessage,
        saveIncomingMessage: saveIncomingMessage
};
```

Integrating the Model into the App

As you have modularized your application into multiple files, you need to import the model file you just created in app.js. To do so, add the following snippet of code after your initial require statements. The bold highlight shows the line added to the previous app.js:

```
var restify = require ('restify');
var builder = require ('builder');
var request = require ('request');
var search = require ('./search');
var model = require('./model');
```

Next you need to add two event listeners; one event listener should be triggered whenever you receive a message from any user to your bot, and the second event listener should be triggered whenever the bot sends a message to the user. Botbuilder emits these two events automatically; you just need to add the handler functions for these functions. In app.js, you will add the two event listeners toward the end of the file, making sure you append the code in app.js.

```
bot.on ('incoming', function(data) {
        model.saveIncomingMessage (data);
        console.log ('-incoming message-');
});

bot.on('outgoing', function(data) {
        model.saveSentMessage (data);
        console.log ('-outgoing message-');
});
```

bot emits the two events named incoming and outgoing on each message received or sent. You have added your event listeners that call the function you had defined in model.js to save the message accordingly. You might be wondering what the data looks like for each case. Well, you should log the data to see what it looks like. The following is the data for incoming messages. You should log the data on the standard output using console.log to see how the payload looks when you are sending a message.

```
{
  "type": "message",
  "timestamp": "2017-08-28T06:03:35.9092036Z",
  "textFormat": "plain",
  "text": "HEy",
  "textLocale": "en-GB",
  "sourceEvent": {
    "clientActivityId": "1503900130494.4429384200782791.8"
  },
  "attachments": [],
  "entities": [],
  "address": {
    "id": "1deef1cc612b4bc181c6449a94a52417|0000007",
    "channelId": "webchat",
    "user": {
      "id": "HtFISdImqn",
      "name": "You"
    },
    "conversation": {
      "id": "1deef1cc612b4bc181c6449a94a52417"
    },
    "bot": {
      "id": "cbbooktest@qVEjtpz7vWc",
      "name": "chatbot-book-test"
    },
    "serviceUrl": "https://webchat.botframework.com/"
  },
  "source": "webchat",
  "agent": "botbuilder",
  "user": {
    "id": "HtFISdImqn",
    "name": "You"
  }
}
```

Now you have the infrastructure to support a bot and the ability to track the messages for further analytics and to understand the usage patterns. You can add your own functionality to the bot by defining your own intents and entities on LUIS.ai and just plug in the business logic code in app.js.

Building Your Own Intent Classifier

In the previous section, you built a chatbot and used LUIS.ai to handle the natural language queries presented by the user. LUIS.ai provides an abstraction ovser a set of machine learning algorithms to power your queries. In this section, you will build a small intent classifier that can be plugged into any chatbot. Developing an intent classifier will help you understand how LUIS.ai or any NLP engine works and will help you better train your bots. Our notion is not to replace LUIS.ai but to supplement the usage of LUIS.ai by covering how to build an intent classifier.

To keep the setup simple and focus on building an intent classifier, you will start a new project and do the development from scratch. It is left to you to integrate the classifier into the bot that you built in the previous section.

What Is a Classifier?

A *classifier* is a computer program that can classify given input into existing/predefined buckets. Wikipedia defines a classifier as follows:

> *An algorithm that implements classification, especially in a concrete implementation, is known as a classifier. The term "classifier" sometimes also refers to the mathematical function, implemented by a classification algorithm, that maps input data to a category.*

You will build your classifier by following a proven statistical model called the naïve Bayes algorithm. For training your classifier, you will need a corpus of labeled data. For this example, the labeled data must be in the following format:

<utterance>,<label>

Before getting into the code implementation and usage, you need an understanding of the naïve Bayes algorithm. The naïve Bayes algorithm is a simple probabilistic classifier based on applying the Bayes theorem with strong independence assumptions between the features. It is a popular method for text categorization, and intent classification is a great fit for problems that can be solved by the naïve Bayes algorithm. The algorithm was introduced under a different name into the text retrieval community in the early 1960s.

The Bayes theorem was named after Thomas Bayes, and it works on conditional probability. Conditional probability is the probability that something will happen given that something else has already happened. You try to use prior knowledge to predict the probability of current event. Here is the formula for calculating the conditional probability:

$$P(H|E) = \frac{P(E|H) * P(H)}{P(E)}$$

where:

- P(H) is the probability of hypothesis H being true. This is known as *prior probability*.

- P(E) is the probability of the evidence (regardless of the hypothesis).

- P(E | H) is the probability of evidence given that the hypothesis is true.

- P(H | E) is the probability of the hypothesis given that the evidence is there.

The naïve Bayes classifier uses the Bayes theorem to predict the membership probability of each feature. The class with the highest probability is considered as the most likely class, which is known as Maximum A Posteriori (MAP). The formula used for calculating MAP (the hypothesis) is given here:

```
MAP (H) = max ( P(H | E)) = max ( (P(E | H) * P(H))/P(E)) = max( P(E | H) * P(H))
```

■ **Note** You can assume that every word in a sentence is independent of the other ones.

The naïve Bayes algorithm is a fast and highly scalable algorithm. It is simple to implement and is a great choice for text classification problems. It is extensively used in the spam detection of e-mails. The good part of the algorithm is that it can be trained on a small data set. One drawback of the algorithm is that it considers all features to be unrelated; hence, it cannot predict the relationship between features. You can improve the accuracy of the naïve Bayes algorithm by doing preprocessing on the data. A good practice is to remove stop-words before running through the classifier. *Stop-words* are common words that don't add any value to the categorization; they are words such as *a, able, either, else, ever,* and so on. Another cleaning technique that is applied is called *lemmatization*. In lemmatization, you find the root word to train your model of a given sentence. Experts have reported that the accuracy of the algorithm can be increased by using TF-IDF instead of a mere count of each word. TF-IDF stands for Term Frequency-Inverse Document Frequency, so instead of counting the frequency of each word, you do more advanced processing like penalizing the more frequently appearing words in the training data.

By now, you have a theoretical understanding of the naïve Bayes algorithm. Let's go ahead and build your own classifier now and see how it performs compared to LUIS.ai.

Coding a Classifier

You will start fresh, so let's create a new project folder called my-classifier and bootstrap the project using NPM.

```
$ mkdir my-classifier
$ cd my-classifier
$ npm init .
```

Give all the defaults when the init command is run for NPM. You will not implement the naïve Bayes classifier but use it from a Node module. The reason to do this is to avoid any errors while building your mathematical model. In machine learning, coming up with the algorithm and doing the feature engineering is more valuable than implementing the algorithm.

■ **Tip**   Always use the implementations of machine learning algorithms that have been open sourced and tested by a number of organizations and people. Implementing an algorithm might not give the best results because of less testing and the introduction of bugs. Also, the machine learning code you write might not be optimized for scale.

For building your naïve Bayes classifier, you will be using the Natural library, which has an open source implementation of the algorithm. The Natural library is available on NPM and is a general language facility for Node. It provides the following as part of its offerings:

- Tokenizing
- Stemming
- Classification
- Phonetics
- TF-IDF
- WordNet
- String similarity

Installing Natural

Let's install the Natural module through NPM. Run the following command in your Terminal window/command prompt:

```
$ npm install --save natural
```

Classifier Module

As discussed in previous sections, we are big fans of modularizing the code into multiple files to make it easy to export the functionality and increase code reuse instead of duplicating the code. Let's create classifier.js in the my-classifier directory.

Your classifier should have support for the following functionality:

- Load and save a classifier file from/to the file system or database for data that has been trained. You do not want to have to train the model every time you start the application.

- Provide APIs to add training on the go. The API can be in the form of function calls.

- Provide a prediction API to return the results that will be a list of probable classification with the confidence for each classification.

From the previous requirements, you can easily conclude that you need the following functions to be implemented in your classifier.js file:

- saveClassifier

- loadClassifier

- addTraining

- predict

Let's implement these functions in your classifier.js file and export them as a module to be consumed by other applications.

classifier.js

```
var natural = require('natural');

function getNewClassifier () {
    return new natural.BayesClassifier();
}

function loadClassifier (sourceFile) {
    return new Promise (function(resolve, reject) {
        natural.BayesClassifier.load (sourceFile, null, function(err,
        loadedClassifier) {
            if (loadedClassifier) {
                return resolve(loadedClassifier);
            } else {
                reject (err);
            }
        });
    });
}
```

```
function saveClassifier (classifier, destinationFile) {
    return new Promise(function (resolve, reject) {
        classifier.save (destinationFile, null, function(err,
        savedClassifier) {
            if (savedClassifier) {
                return resolve (savedClassifier);
            } else {
                return reject (err);
            }
        });
    });
}

function addTraining (classifier, utterance, label) {
    classifier.addDocument (utterance, label);
}

function train(classifier) {
    return new Promise (function (resolve) {
        classifier.train ();
        return resolve ();
    });
}

function predict (classifier, utterance) {
    return JSON.stringify(classifier.classify(utterance));
}

module.exports = {
    loadClassifier: loadClassifier,
    saveClassifier: saveClassifier,
    addTraining: addTraining,
    predict: predict,
    train: train,
    getNewClassifier: getNewClassifier
};
```

You have now built an easy-to-use API over the Natural library. Along with the previously mentioned four functions, you have implemented two extra functions (train, getNewClassifier) to enable the training of current intents and the fetching of a new classifier when no classifier exists. Let's go ahead and use these functions for training a few intents and predicting them after that. Create a file called app.js in the root directory of the my-classifier project.

```javascript
app.js
var mlModel = require('./classifier');

function trainModel () {
    var myClassifier = mlModel.getNewClassifier();
    mlModel.addTraining(myClassifier, "Hello! How are you?", "greeting");
    mlModel.addTraining(myClassifier, "Hi", "greeting");
    mlModel.addTraining(myClassifier, "Hey", "greeting");
    mlModel.addTraining(myClassifier, "What's up", "greeting");
    mlModel.addTraining(myClassifier, "How are you?", "greeting");
    mlModel.addTraining(myClassifier, "I want to buy a shirt", "buy-shirt");
    mlModel.addTraining(myClassifier, "I am looking for shirts", "buy-
    shirt");
    mlModel.addTraining(myClassifier, "Do you have any shirts?", "buy-
    shirt");
    mlModel.addTraining(myClassifier, "Help", "help");
    mlModel.addTraining(myClassifier, "Main Menu", "help");
    mlModel.saveClassifier(myClassifier, 'classifier.json');
}

function loadModel () {
    return new Promise(function(resolve, reject){

        mlModel.loadClassifier('classifier.json').then(function(classifier){
            console.log ('Classifier Loaded');
            mlModel.train(classifier).then(function () {
                console.log ('Model is trained');
                console.log (`Hey!: ${mlModel.predict(classifier,"Hey")}`);
                console.log (`Do you have shirts?: ${mlModel.
                predict(classifier,"I need help looking for shirts")}`);
                return resolve();
            });
        }, function (){
            console.log ('Could not load the Model');
            return reject();
        });
    });
}

loadModel().then(() => {
   console.log ('Finished Execution');
}, () => {
   console.log ('Error with Execution');
});
```

Add the following intents to train by your naïve Bayes classifier:

- Greeting

- Buy-shirt

- Help

Before running the previous `app.js` file, make sure you have run the file when just calling the `trainModel` function. It creates an empty classifier, adds the training data to it, and then finally saves it in a file in the project root directory `classifier.json`. When you call the `loadModel` function, the `classifier.json` file is loaded from the file system, and a classifier is built from it. You then move forward to predict the intents of test data.

■ **Tip** It is a good idea to expose this classifier an API using the Restify module and use the same in the chatbot you built in the previous section. You can compare the results from LUIS.ai and see which one is faring well with added data. Play around with the Natural library and explore the Linear Regression classifier as well.

Summary

Congratulations on completing the longest chapter in the book! You now have gone through the complete life cycle of bot development, starting from coming up with an idea for the chatbot to designing various services around it and finally to putting everything together for a bot to function. Using Botframework, you can deploy the chatbot across various platforms and distribute it to your right target group. Toward the end of the chapter, we covered some advanced topics such as storing the messages for analytics and building your own intent classifier.

CHAPTER 5

■ ■ ■

Business and Monetization

Everything not saved will be lost.

—Nintendo "Quit Screen" message

It has been an exciting journey—we have gone through all the technical aspects of building a chatbot. In the previous chapter, you focused on end-to-end bot building with integrations to a third-party API, connecting to multiple services, and finally deploying it on Facebook Messenger, Skype, and Slack.

In this chapter, we will address the elephant in the room: building a business using chatbots that leverage artificial intelligence and provide value to users. One of the most important steps toward monetizing a nascent technology is to build great analytics. Unless the usage patterns and basic analytics can be tracked, it is hard to understand what your users like or dislike.

We start the chapter by going through the analytics that you should track. Next, we explain where chatbots can play a big role to provide convenience to users. We explore various use cases across many verticals and industries to show examples of where you can put chatbots to good use.

■ **Tip** The best business ideas and solutions are often the result of a person having a hard time performing an activity that should be straightforward. It is a good exercise to pause here and list all the problems you have faced online and offline when communicating with a business or brand; then see if any of those problems can be solved using chatbot technology and data.

Analytics: Why and How?

Data is paramount in today's world; it helps us make better and well-informed decisions. In fact, the largest technology companies around the world have built their dominance because of the data they have. Google indexes the whole World Wide Web for people to search. Facebook has information about most of our friends and family and provides an easy way to be social online. Data speaks volumes about the application usage and usually is an indicator of success when interpreted and worked upon.

Analytics is the science of extracting patterns, trends, and actionable information from the data available. The amount of data generated each year on the Internet has been growing exponentially and can be attributed to three main factors: bandwidth, digital storage, and processing power. The data that is available must be harnessed and analyzed, which will help you keep your brand ahead of disruptions. It can also help you augment your competitive position relative to others in the market you operate in.

As your business starts growing, there are a few metrics that should be constantly monitored to help you mark your progress on a weekly or monthly basis. For consumer-facing businesses, these metrics include the number of active users, returning users, average time spent on the application, and so on. For business-facing businesses, the most common metric to measure is the net promoter score (NPS). Tools that can help you measure these metrics include Google Analytics, Piwik, FireStats, and so on.

Chatbots are at a nascent stage right now, and the toolkit ecosystem around measuring the growth of chatbots is not mature yet. Existing analytics solution such as Google Analytics cannot be used because the metrics required to measure the success criteria of chatbots varies a lot on web or mobile-based applications. Here are a few key differences between traditional (web and mobile) and messaging applications:

- Chat is asynchronous in nature. The number of sessions per user is high, but the average time spent per session is drastically lower. This is because the user messages and returns to what they were doing and then checks for response later.

- Chat works well in customer support use cases, and in these cases the number of returning users will be less because most likely the user's query will be resolved in a single conversation.

- Drop-offs might happen because of various reasons, and page tracking will not be of much help. You need to track the messages where the drop-off is happening and mine the pattern.

To overcome these challenges, you require a stand-alone conversational analytics module that can handle the complexity of measuring the growth of your chatbot. In the next section, we will go through the analytics that are required to follow your success trajectory.

In the previous chapter, you set up your chatbot application to store the messages that are exchanged between the user and the chatbot. You added an event handler that gets triggered on every message that is sent or received by the chatbot. In the next few sections, you will focus on understanding the metrics that play a big role in the success of a chatbot; most of these can be easily tracked from the data you are pushing to MongoDB.

Top Analytics

For you as a brand to gain insights and increase the engagement on your chatbot, you should be tracking certain analytics and metrics irrespective of the type of chatbot. For most of the metrics mentioned here, higher numbers denote the chatbot is doing well.

■ **Tip** When measuring analytics from various key points, the absolute number does not matter. What matters is the relative change in numbers in a defined time frame. Having 100,000 users on a chatbot with that number growing 5 percent a week is much better than having 500,000 users who are constant.

We've chosen some top metrics to cover; they might be different for your business depending on the use case. But if the metrics are changing positively week over week or month over month, you are doing well. In the next sections, we go through the analytics, explain what they mean, and provide a few suggestions from our experience on how to improve upon those metrics.

Number of Users

The total number of users of a chatbot is a good indication of how the bot is perceived by your target group. In most cases, having more users translates to a bot that is providing value to the user. Also, having a large number of users provides the data you need to validate your hypothesis about certain metrics; also, having lots of users removes any error or anomaly that might creep in because of a small sample size. The number of users of the chatbot can be considered equivalent to the number of downloads of mobile applications or the number of unique visits on a web site. The metric change when measuring the number of users should keep growing over the chosen time frame.

Acquiring more users is directly correlated with the awareness of your brand or business among your target audience or group. Having a chatbot will help you with your brand awareness because it forms a source of user acquisition channel.

Retention

The other side of the story for any application is the life cycle of an interaction. Retention shows you the "stickiness" of given chatbot. A chatbot with good retention is the one that engages the current audience until they make a transaction. A *transaction* is defined as the action that must be performed by the user that helps the brand/business achieve a metric. For example, for an e-commerce chatbot, the transaction is defined as a user purchasing an item, whereas for a movie-booking chatbot, the transaction is defined as the user finally booking the movie.

A good retention strategy is to keep retargeting the users based on their usage patterns. If with an e-commerce chatbot a user has looked at a couple of products and has dropped off after that, a good way to engage with the user would be to send a gentle reminder message and show similar items along with it. For a chatbot that provides a mechanism to book tickets to an event, good retention strategies would be to send updates of the event over messaging and to keep the user engaged by sending a quiz or a fact about the event. Your retention strategy will play a big role in keeping your users happy. If a bot sends out too many messages or updates in a day, it might be marked as spam or annoy the users.

■ **Tip**   Provide users with a way to opt out of receiving updates in an accessible way.

Sentiment

Sentiment analysis helps you understand the feelings of the users while using the chatbot. You should always be aiming to provide your customers with a very happy feeling while interacting with your chatbot. Getting stuck in a loop and not being able to understand what the bot is trying to say are the most common ways to have the sentiment of the user go negative.

Design your user experience in a way where if a user gets stuck at any point or is not able to proceed, the user sees navigation options to get back to the main menu or possibly resume the action being performed. Sentiment analysis allows you to solve a problem using a large amount of tagged sentiment data. It is possible to find the training set for you to train your model and employ the naïve Bayes algorithm to get the user's sentiment for each message. Having more negative and neutral feedback than positive is a red flag, in which case you should spend some time focusing on the user journey.

Once a negative sentiment is detected by the chatbot, it is a good idea to let the user know they are being heard and take measures to transfer the chat to a human agent who can assist further in the conversation. The sentiment of the user can be captured through a machine learning model, as discussed earlier, that is implicit (Figure 5-1). Explicit user feedback on the chatbot can also help identify the sentiment, as shown in Figure 5-2.

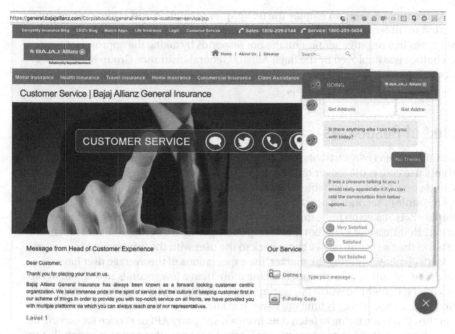

Figure 5-1. *Bajaj Allianz General Insurance chatbot with feedback functionality to capture sentiment explicitly*

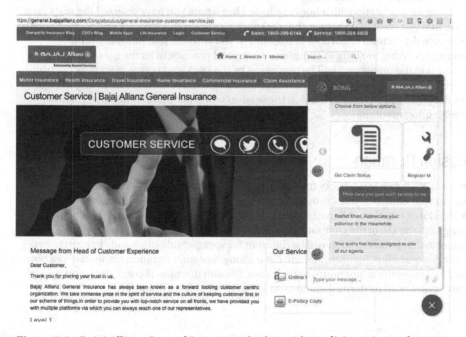

Figure 5-2. *Bajaj Allianz General Insurance chatbot with implicit sentiment detection*

As mentioned, you can employ the techniques of implicit and explicit sentiment detection to understand user behavior. As shown in Figure 5-1 and Figure 5-2, as soon as a user types in a negative sentiment, the bot responds by taking the appropriate action. This chatbot was deployed by the Bajaj Allianz General Insurance Group in India and can be accessed at `https://general.bajajallianz.com/Corp/aboutus/general-insurance-customer-service.jsp`.

Speed of Responses

One of the reasons why chatbots have an edge over normal person-to-person chat in a business use case is the longer time it takes for a human to comprehend what the user has said and come up with a suitable response. A human agent responding to one message takes a couple of seconds if not talking to anyone else. If the human agent is handling multiple chats at a given time, the average turnaround time shoots to more than a few minutes. In the case of a chatbot that is responding to user queries, it should ideally not take more than a second or two to get back to the user with the information requested.

With chatbots entering the market, the expectations of the average user have gone drastically up. If your chatbot is taking more than a few seconds to respond to the user's query, it might be worth taking time out to understand the reason. If your bot is performing an action that is time intensive, it is always a good idea to let the user know about this. If you are trying to fetch data from a third-party API or service for serving the data to the chatbot, it is a good practice to let the user know this and always handle the edge cases wherein the API fails; in other words, provide a suitable error message to the user letting them know the issue.

Imagine a scenario with a booking-based bot where you have selected the seats for a movie that you want to go to over the weekend. The seat-booking back end is overloaded, and hence the chatbot is not able to respond to you with the seat numbers. If the operation is taking too long to complete, it is a good practice to let the user know that the request is in the queue and will be processed by the back-end server as soon as possible. If such a message is not provided, then the user might think there is something wrong with the chatbot and would abandon the session and make another booking request through other medium.

Session Duration

The session duration is a tricky metric to handle. The user should be spending more time on your chatbot while doing something productive. If the user is getting stuck and taking a lot of time between two consecutive interactions, it means there is something wrong with the UX of the chatbot. Session duration alone cannot be linked with a conclusion. Session duration will be different for specific industries and circumstances. An e-commerce bot, for example, will have a longer session duration compared to a bot that gives users the temperature in their area. Session duration is contextual, and no inferences should be derived alone from large/small session duration.

Intent Analytics

Capturing the intent data is important for both the business and the bot developer. As intents directly correlate to the actions performed by the user in the chatbot, intent analytics give a good measure of the top services and actions being performed in the chatbot. As a business, by monitoring the intents being performed in the chatbot, you will have a strategic edge over your competitors. Intent analytics point to the most popular and unpopular services. By optimizing your resources and giving the best experience for popular services, you can increase the retention and overall number of users.

At the end of the day, as the chatbot developer, you should know the top actions being performed by the users on your chatbot. Also, noting the time at which these actions are performed usually provides a lot of information about the chatbot usage.

Capturing the "none" intent is as important as capturing any other intent. The "none" intent frequency will give you the details of how well the NLP on your chatbot works. Typically, a chatbot with excessive "none" intents is most likely an ill-performing bot, with all other analytics data pointing to its demise. It is a good design practice to send out error messages and gracefully handle the situation.

Gender and Age

User profiling helps in understanding your user base. Gender and age play a big role in determining how to market the chatbot to the intended audience. The way to reach each gender and age group is different, and different marketing mechanisms must be applied to capture the audience. Out of the box, Facebook provides some of the user information such as the gender and age group range, whereas on other platforms, it might be worthwhile to collect the same information.

This profiling will also help you as a business to correlate the usage pattern across the different genders and age groups. For an e-commerce chatbot, the age group tagging of each user will help you understand the actions of the various age groups better.

Region

For most use cases, you will define the geography of the chatbot to be launched. It is a good practice to track the location of the chatbot user to get insights into the user's usage pattern across multiple geographies. If you are launching a chatbot that will be used across multiple regions, make sure you provide language support for all the regions.

We've covered the basic set of analytics that you can use to derive value-added insight for you as a chatbot developer or for your brand or business. The rate of growth and adoption of your chatbot is a good metric to keep in mind when building a business-to-consumer (B2C) use case.

Chatbot Use Cases

To a man with a hammer, everything looks like a nail.

—Mark Twain

The chat interface is one of the simplest user interfaces ever designed. It consists of a few message bubbles on either side of a window and a text input area at the bottom of the screen. For a person or organization that is exploring chatbot use cases, it might seem like the chat interface can solve all the problems faced by a user on "regular" user interfaces. In fact, the chat interface feels very natural to us, as our brains are already tuned to how a chat works, thanks to WhatsApp, which has played a major role in the adoption of chat as a channel for peer-to-peer communication.

Chat can disrupt the interfaces that have existed for centuries, and it seems more possible now than ever due to the advancement of technology in machine learning and artificial intelligence. The chat interface wins over any other interface when the function to be performed is specific or can be narrowed down to a specific option in a couple of steps. A few examples where chat can outperform any other user interface are raising a ticket for an issue, requesting past data, and making utility bill payments.

In this section of the chapter, we will go through various modes of communication that exist in today's world, and after that we will cover use cases in every vertical/sector. There are already chatbots being used today in these various use cases.

Modes of Communication

A person often wears multiple hats throughout the day. In this section, we will cover the various roles a person plays throughout the day and show how a person interacts with others in the ecosystem. You will then be in a better position to understand various use-case scenarios where chatbots can be deployed.

Business-to-Business (B2B)

Businesses are usually represented by one person in small organizations or by a group of people in larger organizations. A business typically interacts with other businesses in its domain or outside of its domain for multiple reasons. A business might be procuring some products/services from other business for its day-to-day operation. Chatbots in the form of digital assistants can be deployed in such use cases, wherein the chatbot handles the communication for the business providing the products or services. The assistant can provide information such as opening and closing times, location of various offices, product information, contact information, and so on.

Business-to-Consumer (B2C)

In most use cases, a business is directly providing its products and services to consumers. The frequency of consumers using the service differs depending upon the type and geography of the business. One of the most common examples of a chatbot for a B2C use case is an e-commerce chatbot. An e-commerce chatbot provides all the product and service information about the business. In some cases, consumers might be interested in other uses such as asking about pricing, registering a ticket for a product that was damaged or not delivered on time, and so on.

Consumer-to-Consumer (C2C)

People interacting with other consumers over chat would fall under this category. These are the conversations that are quite hard to automate, and chatbots at this point in time do not seem very useful. In selected scenarios, a chatbot might be employed to increase the quality of conversation. Such scenarios typically fall under a social shopping category. More messaging platforms need to emerge and provide more capabilities to enable the social experience seamlessly.

Business-to-Employee (B2E)

In recent years, the channels through which a business can talk to its employees have opened. The emergence of private social networks can be attributed to the rise of such interactions. A lot of the interaction between the employees and the organization can be automated through chatbots. Popular applications include having a full-blown chatbot for HR-related queries that is plugged into the main HR system. Such chatbots reduce the back and forth when getting to know HR policies, requesting vacation time, and so on.

Employee-to-Employee (E2E)

With the rise of technologies such as Slack, Skype for Business, and Microsoft Teams, employee-to-employee conversations have increased on the chat medium. These products provide support for bots out of the box, which means today there is a big opportunity for build applications that increase the productivity of employees in an organization.

Chatbots by Industry Vertical

We will now focus on verticals and discuss what kind of chatbot scenarios can be built. We will primarily be focusing on B2C verticals because they are very well defined and there is a big scope of problems to be solved. Today, just the customer support market's revenue is more than $20 billion. In most of the section, we cover multiple use cases because it is natural that a brand will have one chatbot that provides both product recommendations and customer support to users.

Banking, Financial Services, and Insurance (BFSI)

The way we have been interacting with our banks and insurance companies has been changing drastically. The BFSI sector is a pioneer in the adoption of new technology. Previously, we either had to visit a bank branch or contact our relationship manager even to request a new checkbook. Today, all these services are just a click away on a web site or mobile app. The next wave of technology adoption has already started by some of the largest banks and insurance companies in the world, wherein they are adopting chatbots for specific use cases and deploying them on a large scale. Let's see the applications that are popular in the BFSI sector.

Internet Banking

Normal banking processes can be accessed over a chat interface, including activities such as finding a branch nearby, checking a balance, requesting a money transfer to another account, and so on (see Figure 5-3). Customer support use cases such as requesting a new card or blocking a stolen credit card can be done easily through a chatbot. The chatbot directly interfaces with the current back-end system of the banking system and is provided with the right permissions to perform actions on the user's behalf.

Figure 5-3. *Bajaj Allianz General Insurance chatbot on Facebook Messenger helping user find a nearby branch*

Insurance

Insurance activities involve a lot of back and forth between the customer and the insurance company. The data that is exchanged between the two parties for most of the interaction is structured and can be automated. Some of the use cases where we have seen the adoption of chatbots in insurance domain are registering an insurance claim, finding out the status of claim, and getting information about other insurance products. In addition, chatbots provide the ability to the company to cross-sell various other products based on the buying pattern of the user. This is one place where the analytics that we discussed at the start of the chapter come in handy. Understanding and building the buying pattern will enable the company to leverage existing data to better suggest products to the user. The second use case where a chatbot can help a user is to decide the right plan based on some initial questions. Frequently users are unaware of the offerings they might be eligible for, and chatbots can help drive sales higher by capturing and utilizing the sales data.

Travel: Booking Bots

Travel is a big market where a lot of customer interaction takes place before a sale is made. One of the major drivers of a sales in the travel space is the price; users are always looking to optimize the price they pay when booking a hotel or flight. Companies such as Skyscanner and Hipmunk provide real-time prices of flights and hotels. One use case would be to integrate and build a chatbot that talks to a couple of back ends to get flight and hotel pricing and keeps tabs of all the prices. As soon as the pricing of certain seat goes up or down, a notification can be triggered. The advantage of chat is that all the context of previous searches is visible on the first screen, and any changes on them can be tracked easily. On the app or web site, as soon as you close and reopen the web site/app, a new context loads with your prior history not easily visible.

Another use case that can be integrated on a chatbot is that of recommending places to visit or see while on a vacation (see Figure 5-4). We often tend to do a lot of searches across multiple blogs to find the right things to do in a city that we visit. Most often, these recommendations are old or are too clichéd. A chatbot can overcome this problem by crowdsourcing the data for a given city. Users provide the latest information about a place, and the chatbot collates all the recommendations and presents them to the user as needed.

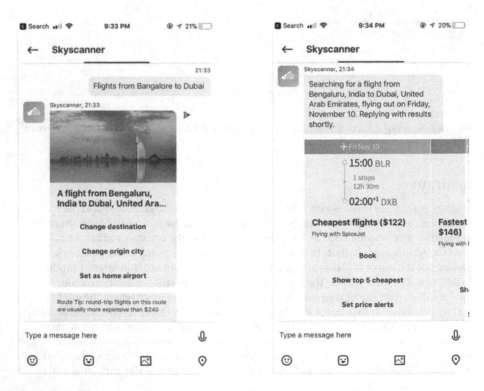

Figure 5-4. *Skyscanner chatbot on Skype that helps user book travel tickets*

Food and Restaurant

We have seen a lot of use cases that can be automated on top of a chatbot in the food industry. These are simple-to-use and simple-to-build use cases, and we urge you to try building one of the chatbots described in this section. One of the major categories of queries for the food industry is related to table reservations; even today most table reservations are handled over a phone. A chatbot seems like a good fit for this problem; it could be convenient to access a chatbot and book a table for any number of people while on the go.

In our experience of building chatbots for more than two years, we have come across a few interesting scenarios for chatbots in the food industry. One of our clients wanted a Bartender Bot, which is live today. The user enters some ingredients into chatbot, and the chatbot then suggests various cocktails that can be made. Along with the suggestions, the chatbot provides the recipes of how to make the cocktails. The major challenge in building this kind of chatbot is the source of data. If the data is available to you and can be consumed by a computer program, though, you can easily convert that data into a beautiful chatbot.

E-commerce

In the use cases for e-commerce, there are primarily two functions that a chatbot can perform: product search and customer support (see Figure 5-5).

Automating customer support for e-commerce is a huge market, and with the advances in the language understanding of computers, soon all customer support queries will be handled by automated systems. Automating the support for level 0 or level 1 type of use cases can be done by a chatbot. The ticketing system can be integrated in the chatbot, which can then be exposed to users.

Figure 5-5. *The Simi Bartender Bot (left), which helps users find recipes about cocktails. On the right is an e-commerce built by Yellow Messenger, which helps users find information from multiple marketplaces (Amazon, Flipkart, and so on).*

Utilities and Bills

Utility services are used by everyone, and paying bill is a use case wherein chatbot automation can help (see Figure 5-6). In our experience, chatbots that help users manage their utilities are one of the fastest-growing areas of bots. These bots see good retention and with a few solid integrations can provide a lot of value to the end customer. Telecom companies and electricity companies can benefit by launching a chatbot for their users on various platforms (web site, Facebook, Skype) and provide basic bill fetching services along with the integration of a payment solution.

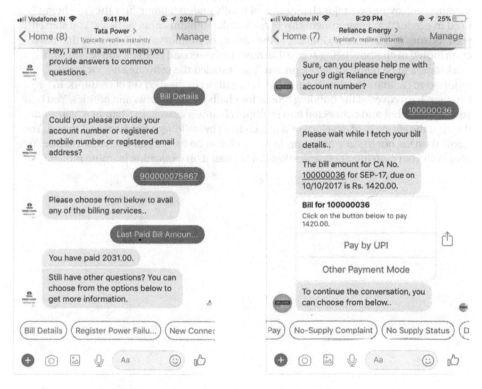

Figure 5-6. *On the left side is the utility chatbot released by Tata Power. On the right is the payment-enabled chatbot by Reliance Energy deployed on Facebook Messenger.*

Summary

In this chapter, we delved deep into the business aspect of chatbots. Chatbots are a very nascent technology that is gaining adoption now because of the advances in machine learning and artificial intelligence. In this chapter, we covered various scenarios where chatbots can make a difference to the user experience today. At the end of the day, as a business, you want to have happy customers and help them achieve more by using your product or service. Chatbots are a way in which users can stay in constant touch with the business/brand, and they provide the business with an opportunity to engage the user easily.

We have finally come to the end of an amazing journey of building chatbots together, deploying on major channels, and finally understanding how they are being used in production environments for brands in different business verticals. You started your journey in this book by looking at the history of chatbots and the factors that have contributed to chatbots being accessible now. In the second chapter, you set up your workstation to be ready for development. You installed the software and packages required to facilitate the development of the chatbots in the next set of chapters. In Chapter 3, we covered the building blocks for chatbots, i.e., intents and entities. You built your first chatbot and connected it to multiple channels as well. In Chapter 4, you went through the life cycle of development of a chatbot by building a bot from end to end. You hooked up the bot to store messages in MongoDB to be used by an analytics module. You also built your own intent classification library based on a machine learning model.

Index

Get the eBook for only $5!

Why limit yourself?

With most of our titles available in both PDF and ePUB format, you can access your content wherever and however you wish—on your PC, phone, tablet, or reader.

Since you've purchased this print book, we are happy to offer you the eBook for just $5.

To learn more, go to http://www.apress.com/companion or contact support@apress.com.

Apress®

Printed in the United States
By Bookmasters